ENRICHING
THE
LITURGY

ENRICHING THE LITURGY

Prayers and Sentences
for the
Common Worship Lectionary

Compiled by
JONATHAN PRIESTLAND YOUNG

First published in Great Britain 1998
Society for Promoting Christian Knowledge
Holy Trinity Church
Marylebone Road
London NW1 4DU

British Library Cataloguing-in-Publication Data

A catalogue record of this book is available from
the British Library

ISBN 0–281–05120–8

Typeset by Pioneer Associates, Perthshire
Printed in Great Britain at
The University Press, Cambridge

Contents

CONTENTS

HOLY DAYS

Foreword by the Archbishop of York

The production of the new *Calendar, Lectionary and Collects*, now approved for use in our Church, gives the opportunity also for the production of other appropriate resource material, both to enhance and enrich the eucharistic celebration.

Already there are within the eucharistic liturgy a number of places where provision is made for flexibility, for the use of 'other suitable words'. In my view, Jonathan Young's compilation is a timely production, resonating well through prayer and Scripture, with the material already provided and authorized for the eucharistic celebration.

In addition to his own altogether more striking and vibrant compilations, he has drawn widely on material from other provinces of the Anglican Communion, and ecumenically, thus drawing into the liturgy the prayer tradition of others with whom we share in the grace of our Lord Jesus Christ and the fellowship of the Holy Spirit.

It strikes me that this production is in the best tradition of liturgical writers both old and new, whereby the interplay between framework and flexibility neither on the one hand promotes 'too much stiffness in refusing' to use a phrase from the preface of the *Book of Common Prayer*, nor on the other 'too much easiness in admitting any variation'.

Above all else, if this material is used sensitively and imaginatively it will surely serve to enable the Church's celebration of the liturgy to draw the worshipper altogether more deeply and profoundly into the mysteries of Christ's own death and resurrection, celebrated and proclaimed in the Eucharist.

† David Ebor

Introduction

This book supplements the provisions of the new *Common Worship* lectionary as published in the *Calendar, Lectionary and Collects*, and authorized by the General Synod of the Church of England for use from Advent 1997. The lectionary itself is a version of the *Revised Common Lectionary*, which over the past twenty-five years has been adopted by Churches of many traditions around the world – Roman Catholic, Anglican, Reformed.

I am grateful to my parishioners and colleagues in the Parish of the Ascension, Cambridge, where we have been using the new lectionary since 1993. In addition to exploring the lectionary and the accompanying collects and post-communion prayers, we have taken the opportunity to develop additional material not provided officially, including new responsorial settings of the psalms and the additional prayers, sentences and acclamations now brought together in Part 1 of this book. Part 2 gives the authorized collects and post-communion prayers for Sundays, seasons and festivals.

This compilation is mainly for use at the Eucharist, although much of the material will be appropriate at family services, Morning and Evening Prayer and other services of the Word, particularly at the main service when the 'principal service lectionary' is used.

The **introductory sentence** is intended for use near the beginning of the service, although it may be found equally suitable at another point. The proposed new eucharistic rite suggests that the president should introduce the liturgy after the opening greeting. The sentence can appropriately follow. At any earlier point, it would be appropriate for an assistant minister to read the sentence, so that the president's first words in the liturgy are the formal liturgical greeting. Alternatively the sentence can be sung by a choir or cantor during the entrance of the ministers or at any appropriate point. Often the sentence anticipates the collect, which is part of the Introduction rather than the Liturgy of the Word.

The **gospel acclamation** is for use before the announcement of the gospel, as suggested in the proposed new rites. Very occasionally the scriptural text is from the appointed gospel reading, but more often it is a related verse from elsewhere in the same gospel or from another part of the Bible. The people should be encouraged to respond 'alleluia!' as indicated in bold type. This should be easy once the custom is established, even when copies of the acclamation are not provided for everyone. During Lent, when by tradition 'alleluia' is not said, an alternative response is provided. This is said first by the reader and repeated by everyone after the biblical text. Alternative lenten responses may be devised, especially when copies of services or of the readings are produced for local use. For principal holy days an alternative extended acclamation is provided. This can also be used where copies are not provided for the people, if the [bracketed] last line is omitted.

The **prayer at the preparation of the table** is for use before the eucharistic prayer. Many of these prayers are not specifically related to the Eucharist and can be used at appropriate points at any service, such as the end of the intercession, the presentation of the collection, or before the blessing and dismissal. At the Eucharist, if there is singing while the elements are prepared, the prayer may be said at the end of the music. Instead of or in addition to these prayers, a prayer may be chosen from another source, such as those provided for general use in the draft new rites.

The **communion sentence** is for use before, during or after the distribution of holy communion. Some of these sentences recall the collect or psalm or one of the readings; more often they anticipate the post-communion prayer. Some are suitable for use at other points during non-eucharistic services.

The material provided should not be used slavishly at the points indicated on every occasion. Rather it is offered as a resource, to draw from as creatively as possible, to enrich the Church's liturgy week by week and day by day.

Jonathan Young

Abbreviations

The sources are indicated by the following initials:

ADK	*All Desires Known*
APB	*Anglican Prayer Book* (1989)
ASB	*Alternative Service Book 1980*
BAS	*Book of Alternative Services*
BCO	*Book of Common Order*
CCP	*Celebrating Common Prayer*
FAS	*For All the Saints*
JPY	original prayer by Jonathan Priestland Young
LHWE	*Lent, Holy Week, Easter: Services and Prayers*
MSB	*Methodist Service Book*
MWV	*Making Women Visible*
NZPB	*A New Zealand Prayer Book*
PBA	*A Prayer Book for Australia*
POHG	*The Promise of His Glory*
PPCW	*Patterns and Prayers for Christian Worship*
URSB	*United Reformed Service Book*
1928PB	*Prayer Book as proposed in 1928*

*An asterisk indicates that the text of a prayer has been amended from the version in the source indicated.

In the case of biblical references, other than the psalms, an asterisk indicates a significant variation from the *New Revised Standard Version of the Bible* or the use of another translation, usually the compiler's own. Minor adaptations of the NRSV text are not indicated. These include the abbreviation of lengthy passages, the substitution of nouns for pronouns and the insertion of words to identify the speaker.

Acknowledgements

Quotations from the Psalms are based on the psalter in *Celebrating Common Prayer*.

Unless otherwise indicated (see note on page xiii), other Scripture quotations are from the *New Revised Standard Version of the Bible*, Anglicized Edition, copyright © 1989, 1995 by the Division of Christian Education of the National Council of the Churches of Christ in the United States of America and are used by permission. All rights reserved.

The compiler and publishers are grateful to the following copyright holders for permission to reproduce material from the sources indicated, some in adapted form (see note on page xiii).

The Central Board of Finance of the Church of England for prayers and acclamations from the *Calendar, Lectionary and Collects*; the *Alternative Service Book 1980*; *Lent, Holy Week, Easter: Services and Prayers*; *The Promise of His Glory* and *Making Women Visible*.

Prayers copied from or based on *For All the Saints*, copyright © 1994, the General Synod of the Anglican Church of Canada. Used with permission.

Prayers copied from or based on the *Book of Alternative Services* of the Anglican Church of Canada, copyright © 1985, the General Synod of the Anglican Church of Canada. Used with permission. The *Book of Alternative Services* was compiled from many pre-existing sources by working committees over a lengthy period of time. Many portions of the text were originally created by the authors.

The Church of the Province of New Zealand for prayers from *A New Zealand Prayer Book, He Karakia Mihinare o Aotearoa* (1989).

The Provincial Trustees of the Church of the Province of Southern Africa for prayers from *An Anglican Prayer Book 1989*.

The Anglican Church of Australia Trust Corporation for prayers from *A Prayer Book for Australia*.

The International Consultation on English in the Liturgy Inc. for prayers based on the *Roman Missal*.

The Panel on Worship of the Church of Scotland for prayers from the *Book of Common Order*.

The United Reformed Church in the United Kingdom for prayers from the *Service Book*.

Prayers from the *Methodist Service Book* © 1975. Used by permission of the Methodist Publishing House.

The Baptist Union for prayers from *Patterns and Prayers for Christian Worship*, adapted by permission.

The European Province of the Society of Saint Francis for prayers from *Celebrating Common Prayer*.

Janet Morley for a prayer adapted from *All Desires Known*.

Prayers from *The Alternative Service Book 1980*; *Lent, Holy Week, Easter* (1986); *The Promise of His Glory* (1991) and *Making Women Visible* (1989) are copyright © The Central Board of Finance of the Church of England and are reproduced by permission.

The compilation of collects and post-communion prayers from the *Common Worship* lectionary, as published in *The Christian Year: Calendar, Lectionary and Collects* (1997), is copyright © The Central Board of Finance of the Church of England, 1995, 1997, and material from it is reproduced with permission. The sources of and details of the copyright holders of the individual collects and post-communion prayers are given on pages 253–64 of *The Christian Year: Calendar, Lectionary and Collects*. Those shown as derived from *The Alternative Service Book 1980*; *Lent, Holy Week, Easter*, 1986; *The Promise of His Glory*, 1991; *Patterns for Worship*, 1995; and *The Prayer Book as Proposed in 1928* (additions and deviations); and as new compositions by the Liturgical Commission of the General Synod of the Church of England, are copyright © The Central Board of Finance of the Church of England, and are reproduced by permission.

Gospel Acclamations for the Church Year are copyright © The Central Board of Finance of the Church of England 1997 and are reproduced by permission.

Part 1
Sentences

The Seasons

Advent

THE FIRST SUNDAY OF ADVENT

INTRODUCTORY SENTENCE

All the tribes of the earth will see the Son of Man coming on
the clouds of heaven with power and great glory.

Matthew 24.30

GOSPEL ACCLAMATION A

Alleluia! **Alleluia!**
Heaven and earth will pass away, says the Lord,
but my words will not pass away. **Alleluia!**

Matthew 24.35

GOSPEL ACCLAMATION B

Alleluia! **Alleluia!**
I have told you this before it occurs, says the Lord,
so that when it does occur, you may believe. **Alleluia!**

John 14.29

GOSPEL ACCLAMATION C

Alleluia! **Alleluia!**
Truly I tell you, says the Lord, there are some standing here
who will not taste death before they see the kingdom of God.
Alleluia!

Luke 9.27

PRAYER AT THE PREPARATION OF THE TABLE

Stir up your power, O God, and come among us;
heal our wounds, calm our fears and give us peace;
through Jesus our Redeemer.

CCP

3

ENRICHING THE LITURGY

COMMUNION SENTENCE

Blessed are those servants whom the master finds alert when
he comes; he will have them sit them down to eat and he
will come and serve them.

Luke 12.37*

—

THE SECOND SUNDAY OF ADVENT

INTRODUCTORY SENTENCE

Prepare the way of the Lord: make his paths straight.

Matthew 3.3

GOSPEL ACCLAMATION A

Alleluia! **Alleluia!**
It is proper for us to fulfil all righteousness. **Alleluia!**

Matthew 3.15*

GOSPEL ACCLAMATION B

Alleluia! **Alleluia!**
The kingdom of God has come near;
repent and believe in the good news. **Alleluia!**

Mark 1.15

GOSPEL ACCLAMATION C

Alleluia! **Alleluia!**
You will be called the prophet of the Most High;
for you will go before the Lord to prepare his ways. **Alleluia!**

Luke 1.76

PRAYER AT THE PREPARATION OF THE TABLE

God of hope, renew in us the joy of your salvation
and make us a living sacrifice to you;
for the sake of Jesus Christ our Lord.

BAS

COMMUNION SENTENCE

Look towards the east, O Jerusalem,
and see the joy that is coming to you from God.

Baruch 4.36

———

THE THIRD SUNDAY OF ADVENT

INTRODUCTORY SENTENCE: *Gaudete*

Rejoice in the Lord always; again I will say, Rejoice.
The Lord is near.

Philippians 4.4–5

GOSPEL ACCLAMATION A

Alleluia! **Alleluia!**
If you are willing to accept it, John is the Elijah who is to
come. Let anyone with ears listen! **Alleluia!**

Matthew 11.14–15

GOSPEL ACCLAMATION B

Alleluia! **Alleluia!** John performed no sign,
but everything that he said about Jesus was true. **Alleluia!**

John 10.41

GOSPEL ACCLAMATION C

Alleluia! **Alleluia!**
The voice of one crying out in the wilderness:
Prepare the way of the Lord. **Alleluia!**

Luke 3.4

PRAYER AT THE PREPARATION OF THE TABLE

Lord our God,
as your servant John the Baptist
prepared the way for the coming of your Son,
make us your servants ready
for his coming in these holy mysteries;
who is alive and reigns now and for ever.

JPY

COMMUNION SENTENCE

Be strong; fear not!
Here is your God; he will come and save you.

Isaiah 35.4*

THE FOURTH SUNDAY OF ADVENT

INTRODUCTORY SENTENCE: *Rorate*

Shower, O heavens, from above
and let the skies rain down righteousness.

Isaiah 45.8

GOSPEL ACCLAMATION A

Alleluia! **Alleluia!**
Joseph was the husband of Mary; of whom Jesus was born,
who is called the Christ. **Alleluia!**

Matthew 1.16

GOSPEL ACCLAMATION B

Alleluia! **Alleluia!**
I am Gabriel; I stand in the presence of God;
and I have been sent to bring you this good news. **Alleluia!**

Luke 1.19

GOSPEL ACCLAMATION C

Alleluia! **Alleluia!**
Greetings, favoured one! The Lord is with you. **Alleluia!**

Luke 1.28

PRAYER AT THE PREPARATION OF THE TABLE

Come, O come, Emmanuel,
you are the way, the truth and the life;
you are the true vine and living bread.
Come, Christ our Saviour,
come to the world which waits for you;
who are alive and reign, now and for ever.

NZPB*

COMMUNION SENTENCE

The young woman is with child and shall bear a son
and shall name him Immanuel.

Isaiah 7.14

Christmas

CHRISTMAS DAY

Any of the alternatives may be used, but it is recommended that the gospel acclamation be chosen according to the set of readings (I, II or III).

INTRODUCTORY SENTENCE

When God brings the firstborn into the world he says,
Let all God's angels worship him.

Hebrews 1.6

or

A child has been born for us, a Son given to us;
authority rests upon his shoulders.

Isaiah 9.6

GOSPEL ACCLAMATION I

Alleluia! **Alleluia!**
I am bringing you good news of great joy for all people.
Alleluia!

Luke 2.10

GOSPEL ACCLAMATION II

Alleluia! **Alleluia!**
Listen, you shepherds; hear the word of the Lord. **Alleluia!**

Ezekiel 34.7*

GOSPEL ACCLAMATION III

Alleluia! **Alleluia!**
We declare to you what was from the beginning,
the Word who is life. **Alleluia!**

1 John 1.1*

EXTENDED ACCLAMATION

Alleluia! **Alleluia!**
Today Christ is born: **Alleluia!**
Today the Saviour has come: **Alleluia!**
Today the angels sing on earth:
Alleluia! [Glory to God in the highest!]

POHG

PRAYER AT THE PREPARATION OF THE TABLE

Heavenly Father,
as your Son was born into the world,
taking our human nature,
may he come again this night/day,
and make known among us his divine glory;
who is alive and reigns, now and for ever.

JPY

or

Son of God, Child of Mary,
born in the stable at Bethlehem,
be born again in us this day,
that through us the world may know
the wonder of your love;
who are alive and reign, now and for ever.

NZPB

COMMUNION SENTENCE

The Word became flesh; we have seen his glory,
full of grace and truth.

John 1.14

or

When the fullness of time had come, God sent his Son, born
of a woman, so that we might receive adoption as children.

Galatians 4.4–5

THE FIRST SUNDAY OF CHRISTMAS

INTRODUCTORY SENTENCE

Let the peace of Christ rule in your hearts;
let the word of Christ dwell in you richly.

Colossians 3.15–16

GOSPEL ACCLAMATION A

Alleluia! **Alleluia!**
Joseph did as the angel of the Lord commanded him.
Alleluia!

Matthew 1.24

GOSPEL ACCLAMATION B

Alleluia! **Alleluia!**
The ox knows its owner and the donkey its master's crib.
Alleluia!

Isaiah 1.3

GOSPEL ACCLAMATION C

Alleluia! **Alleluia!**
The child grew and became strong, filled with wisdom;
and the favour of God was upon him. **Alleluia!**

Luke 2.40

PRAYER AT THE PREPARATION OF THE TABLE

Heavenly Father, tender and compassionate,
by this sacrament create in us your family
    love so true and deep,
that in this broken world we may be a sign of unity;
in your Son Jesus Christ our Lord.

NZPB*

COMMUNION SENTENCE

I pray the Father, from whom every family takes its name,
that you may know the love of Christ and be filled with all
the fullness of God.

Ephesians 3.14–15, 19*

THE SECOND SUNDAY OF CHRISTMAS

INTRODUCTORY SENTENCE

The Word, the true light which enlightens everyone,
was coming into the world.

John 1.9*

GOSPEL ACCLAMATION

Alleluia! **Alleluia!**
The light has come into the world,
and people loved darkness rather than light,
but those who do what is true come to the light. **Alleluia!**

John 3.19, 21

PRAYER AT THE PREPARATION OF THE TABLE

Heavenly Father,
in the mystery of the incarnation
your only-begotten Son shares our human nature,
grant that by the mystery of his body and blood
we may receive his divine life;
who is alive and reigns, now and for ever.

JPY

COMMUNION SENTENCE

Christ Jesus emptied himself, taking the form of a slave,
being born in human likeness.

Philippians 2.7

Epiphany

THE EPIPHANY

6 January

INTRODUCTORY SENTENCE

A bright light will shine to all the ends of the earth;
many nations will come to you from far away,
bearing gifts in their hands for the King of heaven.

Tobit 13.11

GOSPEL ACCLAMATION

Alleluia! **Alleluia!**
The peoples are gathered together and the kingdoms also
to serve the Lord.
Alleluia!

Psalm 102.22

EXTENDED ACCLAMATION

Alleluia! **Alleluia!**
O worship the Lord in the beauty of holiness.
Alleluia!
Tell it out among the nations that the Lord is King.
Alleluia!
Ascribe to the Lord the glory due to his name.
Alleluia!

Psalm 96.9–10; 29.2

PRAYER AT THE PREPARATION OF THE TABLE

Lord Jesus Christ,
to whom the wise men offered their gifts,
as we worship you here on earth
make known in our lives your heavenly glory;
who are alive and reign, now and for ever.

JPY

COMMUNION SENTENCE

We have come with our gifts to worship the Lord.

cf. Matthew 2.2, 11*

THE BAPTISM OF CHRIST

*First Sunday of Epiphany
or Monday 7 January, when 6 January is a Sunday*

INTRODUCTORY SENTENCE

I saw the Spirit descending from heaven like a dove
and it remained on him.

John 1.32

GOSPEL ACCLAMATION A

Alleluia! **Alleluia!**
This is my Son, the beloved: listen to him. **Alleluia!**

Matthew 17.5

GOSPEL ACCLAMATION B

Alleluia! **Alleluia!**
This is the good news about Jesus Christ the Son of God.
Alleluia!

Mark 1.1

GOSPEL ACCLAMATION C

Alleluia! **Alleluia!**
With many exhortations, John the Baptist proclaimed
the good news to the people. **Alleluia!**

Luke 3.18

PRAYER AT THE PREPARATION OF THE TABLE

Open the heavens, Holy Spirit,
for us to see Jesus interceding for us;
may we be willing to share his baptism,
ready to share his cup
and strengthened to serve him for ever.

NZPB*

COMMUNION SENTENCE

Here is the Lamb of God;
I have seen and have testified that this is the Son of God.

John 1.36, 34

THE SECOND SUNDAY OF EPIPHANY

INTRODUCTORY SENTENCE

You know the generous act of our Lord Jesus Christ, that for
your sakes he became poor, so that by his poverty you might
become rich.

2 Corinthians 8.9

GOSPEL ACCLAMATION A

Alleluia! **Alleluia!**
Among you stands one whom you do not know, said John;
the one who is coming after me. **Alleluia!**

John 1.26–27

GOSPEL ACCLAMATION B

Alleluia! **Alleluia!**
Jesus came to Galilee, proclaiming the good news of God.
Alleluia!

Mark 1.14

GOSPEL ACCLAMATION C

Alleluia! **Alleluia!**
Jesus returned to Galilee and a report about him spread
through all the surrrounding country. **Alleluia!**

Luke 4.14

PRAYER AT THE PREPARATION OF THE TABLE

God of life and freedom,
we celebrate the revelation of Jesus
as the Christ who makes all things new:
renew us in him and in our lives make him known,
who is Lord for ever and ever.

BAS*

COMMUNION SENTENCE

Worthy is the Lamb to receive power and wealth and
wisdom and might and honour and glory and blessing!

Revelation 5.12

THE THIRD SUNDAY OF EPIPHANY

INTRODUCTORY SENTENCE

Jesus of Nazareth was attested to you by God with deeds of
power, wonders and signs that God did through him among
you.

Acts 2.22

15

GOSPEL ACCLAMATION A

Alleluia! **Alleluia!**
Jesus went throughout Galilee,
proclaiming the good news of the kingdom. **Alleluia!**

Matthew 4.23

GOSPEL ACCLAMATION B

Alleluia! **Alleluia!**
The fame of Jesus began to spread throughout
the surrounding region of Galilee. **Alleluia!**

Mark 1.28

GOSPEL ACCLAMATION C

Alleluia! **Alleluia!**
All spoke well of Jesus and were amazed at the gracious
words that came from his mouth. **Alleluia!**

Luke 4.22

PRAYER AT THE PREPARATION OF THE TABLE

We pray you, Jesus, take the old water,
our busy conscientious lives,
and turn them into gospel wine,
that everyone who thirsts may see your life;
who are alive and reign, now and for ever.

NZPB*

COMMUNION SENTENCE

The people who walked in darkness have seen a great light.

Isaiah 9.2

THE FOURTH SUNDAY OF EPIPHANY

INTRODUCTORY SENTENCE

It is the God who said, Let light shine out of darkness, who
has shone in our hearts to give the light of the knowledge of
the glory of God in the face of Jesus Christ.

2 Corinthians 4.6

GOSPEL ACCLAMATION A

Alleluia! **Alleluia!**
Jesus was attested to you by God with deeds of power,
wonders and signs. **Alleluia!**

Acts 2.22

GOSPEL ACCLAMATION B

Alleluia! **Alleluia!**
Jesus went throughout Galilee, proclaiming the message in
their synagogues and casting out demons. **Alleluia!**

Mark 1.39

GOSPEL ACCLAMATION C

Alleluia! **Alleluia!**
The Lord has sent me to bring good news to the oppressed.
Alleluia!

Isaiah 61.1

PRAYER AT THE PREPARATION OF THE TABLE

Eternal God,
whose glory was revealed to the world
    in the life of your Son Jesus Christ:
make his life known to us in this most holy sacrament
and grant that our lives in the world may reflect his glory;
who is alive and reigns, now and for ever.

JPY

17

COMMUNION SENTENCE

You are the God who works wonders;
and have declared your power among the peoples.

Psalm 77.14

THE PRESENTATION OF CHRIST
IN THE TEMPLE
(CANDLEMAS)

2 February or the Sunday nearest 31 January

See also The Promise of His Glory, *pp. 272–86.*

INTRODUCTORY SENTENCE

Open for me the gates of righteousness:
I will enter them; I will offer thanks to the Lord.

Psalm 118.19

GOSPEL ACCLAMATION

Alleluia! **Alleluia!**
The true light which enlightens everyone
was coming into the world. **Alleluia!**

John 1.9

EXTENDED ACCLAMATION

Alleluia! **Alleluia!**
Today the Lord is presented in the Temple
in substance of our mortal nature.
Alleluia!
Today the Blessed Virgin comes to be purified
in accordance with the Law.
Alleluia!

Today old Simeon and Anna welcome Christ the redeemer,
the light of the nations, the glory of Israel.
Alleluia! [Praise to Christ the Light of the world!]

POHG*

PRAYER AT THE PREPARATION OF THE TABLE

Heavenly Father,
as your Son Jesus Christ was presented in the Temple,
let our offering today be acceptable to you
and grant that we may see in him, who is our salvation,
the glory of your people and the light of all the nations;
who is alive and reigns, now and for ever.

JPY

COMMUNION SENTENCE

My eyes have seen your salvation, which you have prepared
in the presence of all peoples.

Luke 2.30–31

or

This child is destined for the falling and the rising of many
and to be a sign that will be opposed; and a sword will pierce
your own soul too.

Luke 2.34–35

_____ Ordinary Time _____

The provision for the last two Sundays before Lent is always used (see pages 24–5).

The prayers and sentences of the third, fourth and fifth Sundays before Lent and the lectionary of Propers 1 to 3 are used only as necessary, when there are more than two Sundays between Candlemas and Ash Wednesday.

The following gospel acclamations are provided for use with the lectionary of Propers 1 to 3, according to calendar date.

PROPER 1, Sunday nearest 6 February

GOSPEL ACCLAMATION A

Alleluia! **Alleluia!**
My Father is glorified by this, that you bear much fruit and become my disciples. **Alleluia!**

John 15.8

GOSPEL ACCLAMATION B

Alleluia! **Alleluia!**
A new teaching – with authority he commands even the unclean spirits, and they obey him. **Alleluia!**

Mark 1.27

GOSPEL ACCLAMATION C

Alleluia! **Alleluia!**
I must proclaim the good news of the kingdom of God, for I was sent for this purpose. **Alleluia!**

Luke 4.43

PROPER 2, Sunday nearest 13 February

GOSPEL ACCLAMATION A

Alleluia! **Alleluia!**
A person is justified not by the works of the law,
but through faith in Jesus Christ. **Alleluia!**

Galatians 2.16

GOSPEL ACCLAMATION B

Alleluia! **Alleluia!**
You have been cleansed, says the Lord,
by the word that I have spoken to you. **Alleluia!**

John 15.3

GOSPEL ACCLAMATION C

Alleluia! **Alleluia!**
Blessed are those who hear the word of God and obey it!
Alleluia!

Luke 11.28

PROPER 3, Sunday nearest 20 February

GOSPEL ACCLAMATION A

Alleluia! **Alleluia!**
I am the Lord your God; sanctify yourselves therefore
and be holy, for I am holy. **Alleluia!**

Leviticus 11.44

GOSPEL ACCLAMATION B

Alleluia! **Alleluia!**
Jesus went to Capernaum and they were astounded at his
teaching, for he taught them as one having authority.
Alleluia!

Mark 1.21–22

GOSPEL ACCLAMATION C

Alleluia! **Alleluia!**
As he who called you is holy, be holy yourselves in all your
conduct; for it is written, You shall be holy, for I am holy.
Alleluia!

1 Peter 1.15–16

—

THE FIFTH SUNDAY BEFORE LENT

INTRODUCTORY SENTENCE

May God make you worthy of his call and fulfil by his power
every good resolve and work of faith.

2 Thessalonians 1.11*

PRAYER AT THE PREPARATION OF THE TABLE

Loving God, before the world began you called us:
make our lives holy as we come to you this day
and strengthen us in our calling;
we ask this in the name of Jesus Christ our Lord.

BAS*

COMMUNION SENTENCE

We declare to you what we have seen with our eyes,
what we have touched with our hands,
so that you may have fellowship with us
and with the Father and with his Son Jesus Christ.

1 John 1.1, 3

—

THE FOURTH SUNDAY BEFORE LENT

INTRODUCTORY SENTENCE

The Lord is good, a stronghold on a day of trouble;
he protects those who take refuge in him.

Nahum 1.7

PRAYER AT THE PREPARATION OF THE TABLE

Christ our great high priest, you understand our weakness;
you pray for us while we are sinners;
help us to find a new and living way to God,
through you, who are alive and reign, now and for ever.

NZPB*

COMMUNION SENTENCE

Let your light shine before others, so that they may see your
good works and give glory to your Father in heaven.

Matthew 5.16

THE THIRD SUNDAY BEFORE LENT

INTRODUCTORY SENTENCE

O Lord, I delight in your commandments,
    which I have always loved;
your decrees are my inheritance for ever;
    truly, they are the joy of my heart.

Psalm 119.47, 111

PRAYER AT THE PREPARATION OF THE TABLE

God our sustainer, in this holy sacrament
feed us continually with that bread which satisfies all hunger,
your Son Jesus Christ our Lord.

BAS*

COMMUNION SENTENCE

I am the bread of life, says the Lord.
Whoever comes to me will never be hungry
and whoever believes in me will never be thirsty.

John 6.35

THE SECOND SUNDAY BEFORE LENT

INTRODUCTORY SENTENCE

O Lord, how manifold are your works!
In wisdom you have made them all;
the earth is full of your creatures.

Psalm 104.24

GOSPEL ACCLAMATION A

Alleluia! **Alleluia!**
Your Father in heaven will give good things
to those who ask him. **Alleluia!**

Matthew 7.11

GOSPEL ACCLAMATION B

Alleluia! **Alleluia!**
God has spoken to us by the Son,
through whom he created the worlds. **Alleluia!**

Hebrews 1.2

GOSPEL ACCLAMATION C

Alleluia! **Alleluia!**
Blessed are those who hear the word of God and obey it.
Alleluia!

Luke 11.28

PRAYER AT THE PREPARATION OF THE TABLE

Source of all life, the heaven and the earth are yours,
yet you have given us dominion over all things:
receive these gifts of your creation
which we offer you this day,
in the name of Jesus Christ our Lord.

BAS*

COMMUNION SENTENCE

To everyone who conquers, says the Lord,
I will give permission to eat from the tree of life
that is in the paradise of God.

Revelation 2.7

THE SUNDAY NEXT BEFORE LENT

INTRODUCTORY SENTENCE

When Christ is revealed we will be like him,
for we will see him as he is.

1 John 3.2

GOSPEL ACCLAMATION

Alleluia! **Alleluia!**
The glory of the Lord shall be revealed;
the mouth of the Lord has spoken. **Alleluia!**

Isaiah 40.5

PRAYER AT THE PREPARATION OF THE TABLE

Lord,
as your Son was transfigured before the disciples,
may these gifts be made holy by the splendour of his glory
and our lives be transformed by his presence;
who is alive and reigns, now and for ever.

JPY

COMMUNION SENTENCE

Lord, it is good for us to be here.

Matthew 17.4

_____ Lent _____

ASH WEDNESDAY

INTRODUCTORY SENTENCE

You are merciful to all, O Lord,
and you overlook people's sins so that they may repent;
for you love all things that exist
and detest none of the things that you have made.

Wisdom 11.23–24

GOSPEL ACCLAMATION

Praise and honour to Christ Jesus!
All who exalt themselves will be humbled;
but all who humble themselves will be exalted.
Praise and honour to Christ Jesus!

Luke 18.14

PRAYER AT THE PREPARATION OF THE TABLE

Merciful God,
turn us from sin to faithfulness,
accept our offering
and prepare us to celebrate
the death and resurrection of Christ our Saviour,
who is alive and reigns, now and for ever.

BAS*

COMMUNION SENTENCE

Do not work for the food that perishes, but for the food that
endures for eternal life, which the Son of Man will give you.

John 6.27

THE FIRST SUNDAY OF LENT

INTRODUCTORY SENTENCE

Jesus in every respect has been tempted as we are,
yet without sin.

Hebrews 4.15

GOSPEL ACCLAMATION

Praise and honour to Christ Jesus!
One does not live by bread alone,
but by every word that comes from the mouth of God.
Praise and honour to Christ Jesus!

Deuteronomy 8.3

or

Blessed is anyone who endures temptation;
such a one has stood the test and will receive the crown
of life.

James 1.12

PRAYER AT THE PREPARATION OF THE TABLE

God of the desert, as we follow Jesus into the unknown,
may we recognize the tempter when he comes;
let it be your bread we eat,
your world we serve and you alone we worship;
we ask this through Christ our Lord.

NZPB

COMMUNION SENTENCE

Blessed are those who hunger and thirst for righteousness
for they will be filled.

Matthew 5.6

THE SECOND SUNDAY OF LENT

INTRODUCTORY SENTENCE

Send out your light and your truth; that they may lead me;
and bring me to your holy hill and to your dwelling.

Psalm 43.3

GOSPEL ACCLAMATION A

Praise and honour to Christ Jesus!
Those who do what is true come to the light, says the Lord,
so that it may be clearly seen that their deeds have been
    done in God.
Praise and honour to Christ Jesus!

John 3.21

GOSPEL ACCLAMATION B

Praise and honour to Christ Jesus!
I, when I am lifted up from the earth, says the Lord,
will draw all people to myself.
Praise and honour to Christ Jesus!

John 12.32

GOSPEL ACCLAMATION C

Praise and honour to Christ Jesus!
Out of Zion shall go forth instruction
and the word of the Lord from Jerusalem.
Praise and honour to Christ Jesus!

Isaiah 1.2

PRAYER AT THE PREPARATION OF THE TABLE

Grant, O Lord,
that as we lift up these earthly gifts
in the name of your Son Jesus Christ,
so we may share in the heavenly banquet of his eternal life,
who is alive and reigns, now and for ever.

JPY

COMMUNION SENTENCE

Whoever believes in the Son of Man shall have eternal life.

John 3.15

THE THIRD SUNDAY OF LENT

INTRODUCTORY SENTENCE

The message about the cross is foolishness to those who are perishing, but to us who are being saved it is the power of God.

1 Corinthians 1.18

GOSPEL ACCLAMATION A

Praise and honour to Christ Jesus!
Whoever believes in the Son has eternal life.
Praise and honour to Christ Jesus!

John 3.36

GOSPEL ACCLAMATION B

Praise and honour to Christ Jesus!
you search the scriptures
    because you think that in them you have eternal life;
and it is they that testify on my behalf.
Praise and honour to Christ Jesus!

John 5.39

GOSPEL ACCLAMATION C

Praise and honour to Christ Jesus!
Those who abide in me and I in them bear much fruit,
    says the Lord.
Praise and honour to Christ Jesus!

John 15.5

PRAYER AT THE PREPARATION OF THE TABLE

Almighty God,
your beloved Son, for love of us, willingly offered himself
to endure the cross, its agony and its shame:
give us grace to take up our cross
and to follow him in humility and love;
who is alive and reigns, now and for ever.

BCO*

COMMUNION SENTENCE

My food is to do the will of him who sent me, says the Lord.

John 4.34

THE FOURTH SUNDAY OF LENT

INTRODUCTORY SENTENCE: *Laetare*

Rejoice with Jerusalem and be glad for her,
    all you who love her;
rejoice with her in joy, all you who mourn.

Isaiah 66.10

GOSPEL ACCLAMATION A

Praise and honour to Christ Jesus!
Your word is a lamp to my feet and a light to my path.
Praise and honour to Christ Jesus!

Psalm 119.105

GOSPEL ACCLAMATION B

Praise and honour to Christ Jesus!
I am the light of the world, says the Lord;
whoever follows me will have the light of life.
Praise and honour to Christ Jesus!

John 8.12

GOSPEL ACCLAMATION C

Praise and honour to Christ Jesus!
The Son of Man came to seek out and to save the lost.
Praise and honour to Christ Jesus!

Luke 19.10

PRAYER AT THE PREPARATION OF THE TABLE

God of wisdom,
may the light of the eternal Word,
our Lord and Saviour Jesus Christ,
guide us to your glory;
we ask this in his name.

BAS

COMMUNION SENTENCE

I am the gate, says the Lord; whoever enters by me will come
in and go out and find pasture.

John 10.9

MOTHERING SUNDAY
(The Fourth Sunday of Lent)

INTRODUCTORY SENTENCE: *Laetare*

Rejoice with Jerusalem and be glad for her,
    all you who love her:
rejoice with her in joy, all you who mourn over her;
as a mother comforts her child,
    so I will comfort you, says the Lord:
you shall be comforted in Jerusalem.

Isaiah 66.10, 13

GOSPEL ACCLAMATION

Praise and honour to Christ Jesus!
Whoever does the will of my Father in heaven
is my brother and sister and mother, says the Lord.
Praise and honour to Christ Jesus!

Matthew 12.50

PRAYER AT THE PREPARATION OF THE TABLE

Jesus,
as a mother you gather your people to you,
you comfort us in sorrow and bind up our wounds:
in your compassion bring grace and forgiveness;
and may your love in this sacrament
prepare us for the beauty of heaven;
where you are alive and reign, now and for ever.

MWV*

COMMUNION SENTENCE

Jerusalem, Jerusalem, how often have I desired to gather your
children together as a hen gathers her brood under her
wings, says the Lord.

Matthew 23.37

THE FIFTH SUNDAY OF LENT

INTRODUCTORY SENTENCE

I want to know Christ and the power of his resurrection.

Philippians 3.10

GOSPEL ACCLAMATION A

Praise and honour to Christ Jesus!
The works that I do in my Father's name testify to me,
    says the Lord;
the Father and I are one.
Praise and honour to Christ Jesus!

John 10.25, 30

GOSPEL ACCLAMATION B

Praise and honour to Christ Jesus!
Those who want to save their life will lose it, says the Lord,
and those who lose their life for my sake
   and for the sake of the gospel will save it.
Praise and honour to Christ Jesus!

Mark 8.35

GOSPEL ACCLAMATION C

Praise and honour to Christ Jesus!
God fulfilled what he had foretold through all the prophets,
that his Messiah would suffer.
Praise and honour to Christ Jesus!

Acts 3.18

PRAYER AT THE PREPARATION OF THE TABLE

Living Lord,
the way of your cross is shown to be the way
   of our salvation,
your love and forgiveness are displayed
   as the keys of our redemption
and your sacrificial love is offered as the foundation
   of our hope;
Lord Jesus, help us to follow you,
who are alive and reign, now and for ever.

PPCW*

COMMUNION SENTENCE

The Son of Man came not to be served but to serve,
and to give his life as a ransom for many.

Mark 10.45

Holy Week

PALM SUNDAY

INTRODUCTORY SENTENCE

Hosanna to the Son of David, the King of Israel.
Blessed is he who comes in the name of the Lord.
Hosanna in the highest heaven!

Matthew 21.9, John 12.13

GOSPEL ACCLAMATION

Praise and honour to Christ Jesus!
If any want to become my followers, says the Lord,
let them deny themselves and take up their cross
   and follow me.
Praise and honour to Christ Jesus!

Matthew 16.24; Mark 8.34; Luke 9.23

PRAYER AT THE PREPARATION OF THE TABLE

Lord, may the passion of your only Son make us pleasing
   to you,
that we may gain your mercy and love
not by any merits of our own but by his perfect sacrifice;
we ask this in his name.

JPY from Roman Missal

COMMUNION SENTENCE

Through Christ, God was pleased to reconcile to himself
all things, whether on earth or in heaven,
by making peace through the blood of his cross.

Colossians 1.20

or

34

Jesus said, My Father, if this cup cannot pass unless I drink it,
your will be done.

Matthew 26.42*

MONDAY TO WEDNESDAY IN
HOLY WEEK

Some of the material provided for Palm Sunday is also suitable.

INTRODUCTORY SENTENCE

We adore you, O Christ, and we bless you:
because by your holy cross you have redeemed the world.

Traditional

or

Christ Jesus humbled himself
and became obedient to the point of death –
even death on the cross.

Philippians 2.8

GOSPEL ACCLAMATION

Praise and honour to Christ Jesus!
The hour has come for the Son of Man to be glorified;
Father, glorify your name!
Praise and honour to Christ Jesus!

John 12.23, 28

PRAYER AT THE PREPARATION OF THE TABLE

Lord God,
whose Son is the true vine and the source of life,
ever giving himself that the world may live;
may we so receive within ourselves
the power of his death and passion,
that in this cup of his life we may share his glory
and be made perfect in his love;
who is alive and reigns, now and for ever.

LHWE

35

COMMUNION SENTENCE

Was it not necessary that the Christ should suffer these
things and then enter into his glory?

Luke 24.26

MAUNDY THURSDAY

INTRODUCTORY SENTENCE

Jesus said, I have eagerly desired to eat this Passover
  with you before I suffer;
I will not eat it until it is fulfilled in the kingdom of God.

Luke 22.15–16

GOSPEL ACCLAMATION

Praise and honour to Christ Jesus!
This is my commandment,
that you love one another as I have loved you.
Praise and honour to Christ Jesus!

John 15.12

or

A new commandment I give unto you,
that you love one another, as I have loved you;
by this everyone will know that you are my disciples,
if you have love for one another.

John 13.34–35*

PRAYER AT THE PREPARATION OF THE TABLE

Infinite, intimate God,
this night you kneel before your friends and wash our feet:
bound together in your love, trembling,
we drink your cup and watch with you,
who are alive and reign, now and for ever.

NZPB*

or

God our Father,
your Son Jesus Christ has left to us
  this meal of bread and wine

in which we share his body and his blood:
as we keep the feast of his redeeming love
may we feed on him by faith,
receive his grace and find fullness of life;
through the same Jesus Christ our Lord.

BCO

COMMUNION SENTENCE

As often as you eat this bread and drink the cup,
you proclaim the Lord's death until he comes.

1 Corinthians 11.26

GOOD FRIDAY

*The Good Friday Liturgy customarily begins not with a greeting
or introductory sentence, but a period of silent prayer, followed
immediately by the collect.*

*The **introductory sentence** provided here may be used at non-
liturgical services or at a later point in the Good Friday Liturgy.
For use during the Proclamation of the Cross extended versions
are given in* Lent, Holy Week, Easter, *(pp. 207–10) and in the*
New English Hymnal *(no. 516).*

*The **gradual** is provided instead of the usual gospel acclamation,
for use before the Passion Gospel according to St John.*

*The **prayer at the preparation of the table** may be used if
there is a celebration of the Eucharist or during the Proclamation
of the Cross. It should not be used in connection with the
distribution of elements already consecrated at the Maundy
Thursday Liturgy.*

INTRODUCTORY SENTENCE

O my people, what have I done to you,
in what have I wearied you? Answer me!
For I redeemed you from the house of slavery
that you may know the saving acts of the Lord.

Micah 6.3–5

37

GRADUAL

Christ became obedient to the point of death, even death on
the cross; therefore God also highly exalted him and gave
him the name that is above every name.

Philippians 2.8–9

PRAYER AT THE PREPARATION OF THE TABLE

Lord Jesus Christ,
as we kneel at the foot of your cross,
help us to see and know your love for us,
so that we may place all that we have and all that we are
    at your feet;
who are alive and reign, now and for ever.

NZPB*

COMMUNION SENTENCE

It is written, I will strike the shepherd
and the sheep of the flock will be scattered.

Matthew 26.31

or

Every time you eat this bread and drink this cup,
you proclaim the death of the Lord, until he comes.

1 Corinthians 11.26

EASTER EVE

*The Eucharist is not celebrated on Easter Eve. This material is
provided for non-eucharistic services.*

INTRODUCTORY SENTENCE

We have been buried with Christ by baptism into death,
so that just as he was raised from the dead by the glory
of the Father, so we too might walk in newness of life.

Romans 6.4

GRADUAL

They made his grave with the wicked and his tomb with the
rich, although he had done no violence and there was no
deceit in his mouth.

Isaiah 53.9

ADDITIONAL PRAYERS

We remember, O God,
the grief of the disciples when Jesus died:
lead us beyond our fear of death
to the joyful knowledge of eternal life
in him who is alive and reigns, now and for ever.

NZPB*

O God, creator of heaven and earth,
as the crucified body of your dear Son
was laid in the tomb and rested on this holy Sabbath,
so may we await the coming of the third day
and rise with him to newness of life;
who is alive and reigns, now and for ever.

BAS*

Lord Jesus Christ, Son of the living God,
who on this day lay in the tomb
and so hallowed the grave
    to be a bed of hope for all who put their trust in you:
give us such sorrow for our sins,
which were the cause of your passion,
that when our bodies lie in the dust
our souls may live with you;
who are alive and reign, now and for ever.

CCP*

_____ Easter _____

EASTER DAY

INTRODUCTORY SENTENCE

Christ has been raised from the dead, alleluia!
the first-fruits of those who have died,
alleluia, alleluia, alleluia!

1 Corinthians 15.20

_or_

Alleluia! Christ is risen!
He is risen indeed, alleluia!

cf Luke 24.34*

GOSPEL ACCLAMATION

Alleluia! **Alleluia!**
Give thanks to the Lord for he is good;
his mercy endures for ever. **Alleluia!**

Psalm 118.1

_or_

Alleluia! **Alleluia!**
Our paschal lamb, Christ has been sacrificed;
therefore let us celebrate the festival. **Alleluia!**

1 Corinthians 5.7–8

EXTENDED GOSPEL ACCLAMATION

Alleluia! **Alleluia!**
Christ our passover has been sacrificed for us;
therefore let us keep the feast.
Alleluia!

Christ, once raised from the dead, dies no more.
Alleluia!
Christ has been raised from the dead,
the firstfruits of those who sleep.
Alleluia!
[Thanks be to God, who gives us the victory
through our Lord Jesus Christ!]

1 Corinthians 5.7–8*; Romans 6.9*; 1 Corinthians 15.20, 57*

PRAYER AT THE PREPARATION OF THE TABLE

Holy God,
you feed us with earthly and with spiritual food:
deathless, unalterable,
you have chosen us, sinful as we are,
to hear your word and to proclaim your truth.
Alleluia! Make us salt of the earth;
make us yeast in the loaf;
we ask this in the name of our risen Lord, Jesus Christ.

NZPB

COMMUNION SENTENCE

Those who eat my flesh and drink my blood have eternal life,
says the Lord, and I will raise them up on the last day,
alleluia!

John 6.54

THE SECOND SUNDAY OF EASTER

INTRODUCTORY SENTENCE: *Quasimodo*

Like new born infants, alleluia!
long for the pure spiritual milk, alleluia!
that by it you may grow into salvation, alleluia, alleluia!

1 Peter 2.2

or

Let us celebrate the festival, alleluia!
with the unleavened bread of sincerity and truth,
     alleluia, alleluia!

1 Corinthians 5.8

GOSPEL ACCLAMATION

Alleluia! **Alleluia!**
Peace I leave with you, says the Lord; my peace I give to you.
Alleluia!

John 14.27

or

Alleluia! **Alleluia!**
Blessed are those who have not seen
and yet have come to believe. **Alleluia!**

John 20.29

PRAYER AT THE PREPARATION OF THE TABLE

Lord Jesus Christ,
in baptism you give us your Spirit of forgiveness and peace:
by this sacrament of unity,
     grant us to know your victory over sin and death;
for you are alive and reign, now and for ever.

JPY

COMMUNION SENTENCE

We have been buried with Christ by baptism into death, so
that, just as he was raised from the dead by the glory of the
Father, so we too might walk in newness of life, alleluia!

Romans 6.4

or

Go into all the world and proclaim the good news to the
whole creation; the one who believes and is baptized will
be saved, alleluia!

Mark 16.15–16

THE THIRD SUNDAY OF EASTER

INTRODUCTORY SENTENCE

Jesus came and stood among the disciples, alleluia!
then they rejoiced when they saw the Lord, alleluia, alleluia!

John 20.19–20

GOSPEL ACCLAMATION A

Alleluia! **Alleluia!**
You search the scriptures to find in them eternal life,
says the Lord; it is they that testify on my behalf. **Alleluia!**

John 5.39*

GOSPEL ACCLAMATION B

Alleluia! **Alleluia!**
I will see you again and your hearts will rejoice, says the
Lord, and no one shall take your joy from you. **Alleluia!**

John 16.22

GOSPEL ACCLAMATION C

Alleluia! **Alleluia!**
It is written, I will strike the shepherd and the sheep of the
flock will be scattered. But after I am raised up, says the Lord,
I will go ahead of you to Galilee. **Alleluia!**

Matthew 26.31–32

PRAYER AT THE PREPARATION OF THE TABLE

Lord Jesus, we believe you; all we heard is true;
you break the bread: we recognize you;
you are the fire that burns within us:
　　use us to light the world;
we ask this in your name.

NZPB*

COMMUNION SENTENCE

I am the living bread, says the Lord. Whoever eats of this
bread will live for ever; and the bread that I will give for the
life of the world is my flesh, alleluia!

John 6.51

THE FOURTH SUNDAY OF EASTER

INTRODUCTORY SENTENCE

I am the resurrection and the life, says the Lord, alleluia!
everyone who lives and believes in me will never die,
     alleluia, alleluia!

John 11.25–26

GOSPEL ACCLAMATION

Alleluia! **Alleluia!**
I myself will be the shepherd of my sheep, says the Lord.
Alleluia!

Ezekiel 34.15

or

Alleluia! **Alleluia!**
The Lamb at the centre of the throne will be their shepherd
and he will guide them to springs of the water of life.
Alleluia!

Revelation 7.17

PRAYER AT THE PREPARATION OF THE TABLE

God of loving care,
you spread before us the table of life
and give us the cup of salvation to drink:
keep us always in the fold of our Saviour and our Shepherd,
your Son Jesus Christ our Lord.

BAS*

COMMUNION SENTENCE

The Lord will feed his flock like a shepherd; he will gather
the lambs in his arms and carry them in his bosom, alleluia!

Isaiah 40.11

THE FIFTH SUNDAY OF EASTER

INTRODUCTORY SENTENCE

This is indeed the will of my Father, that all who see the Son
    and believe in him may have eternal life, alleluia!
and I will raise them up on the last day, alleluia, alleluia!

John 6.40

GOSPEL ACCLAMATION A

Alleluia! **Alleluia!**
I have not spoken on my own, says the Lord, but the Father
who sent me has himself given me a commandment about
what to say and what to speak. **Alleluia!**

John 12.49

GOSPEL ACCLAMATION B

Alleluia! **Alleluia!**
You did not choose me but I chose you, says the Lord,
and I appointed you to go and bear fruit, fruit that will last.
Alleluia!

John 15.16

GOSPEL ACCLAMATION C

Alleluia! **Alleluia!**
This is my commandment, says the Lord: that you love one
another, as I have loved you. **Alleluia!**

John 15.12

PRAYER AT THE PREPARATION OF THE TABLE

Gracious God,
you show us your way and give us your divine life:
may everything we do be directed
    by the knowledge of your truth;
we ask this in the name of Jesus Christ our risen Lord.

BAS

COMMUNION SENTENCE

I am the way and the truth and the life, says the Lord;
no one comes to the Father except through me, alleluia!

John 14.6

THE SIXTH SUNDAY OF EASTER

INTRODUCTORY SENTENCE

God has rescued us from the power of darkness, alleluia!
and transferred us into the kingdom of his beloved Son,
    alleluia, alleluia!

Colossians 1.13

GOSPEL ACCLAMATION

Alleluia! **Alleluia!**
A little while and you will no longer see me, says the Lord;
and again a little while and you will see me. **Alleluia!**

John 16.16

PRAYER AT THE PREPARATION OF THE TABLE

Lord Jesus Christ, bread of life,
as we come to you in this supper grant us never to hunger;
grant that, believing in you, we may never thirst;
we ask this in your name, who are alive and reign for ever.

JPY

COMMUNION SENTENCE

Those who drink of the water that I will give them will never
be thirsty; the water that I will give, says the Lord, will
become a spring of water gushing up to eternal life, alleluia!

John 4.14

ASCENSION DAY

INTRODUCTORY SENTENCE: *Viri Galilei*

Men of Galilee,
why do you stand looking up towards heaven? alleluia!
This Jesus, who has been taken up from you into heaven,
will come in the same way as you saw him go into heaven,
    alleluia, alleluia, alleluia!

Acts 1.11

GOSPEL ACCLAMATION

Alleluia! **Alleluia!**
Go and make disciples of all nations, says the Lord,
and remember, I am with you always, to the end of the age.
Alleluia!

Matthew 28.19–20

EXTENDED GOSPEL ACCLAMATION

Alleluia! **Alleluia!**
God has highly exalted Christ Jesus;
Alleluia!
At the name of Jesus every knee shall bow;
Alleluia!
Let every tongue confess that Jesus Christ is Lord;
Alleluia! [Glory to God the Father!]

from Philippians 2.9–11*

47

PRAYER AT THE PREPARATION OF THE TABLE

Lord Jesus Christ, our great high priest,
who promised your disciples to be with them always,
let this sacrament be for us a foretaste of the banquet
    in heaven,
where you are alive and reign, now and for ever.

JPY

COMMUNION SENTENCE

Blessed be the God and Father of our Lord Jesus Christ,
who has blessed us in Christ with every spiritual blessing
    in the heavenly places, alleluia!

Ephesians 1.3

THE SEVENTH SUNDAY OF EASTER

INTRODUCTORY SENTENCE

I will not leave you orphaned, says the Lord, alleluia!
I am coming to you, alleluia, alleluia!

John 14.18

GOSPEL ACCLAMATION

Alleluia! **Alleluia!**
When the Spirit of truth comes,
he will guide you into all truth. **Alleluia!**

John 16.13

PRAYER AT THE PREPARATION OF THE TABLE

Father, by your Holy Spirit,
hold the Church in unity and keep it faithful to your word,
so that, breaking bread together,
we may be one with Christ in faith and love and service,
now and for ever.

PBA

COMMUNION SENTENCE

Go into all the world and proclaim the good news
to the whole creation, alleluia!

Mark 16.15

PENTECOST

INTRODUCTORY SENTENCE

You will receive power, alleluia!
when the Holy Spirit has come upon you,
alleluia, alleluia, alleluia!

Acts 1.8

GOSPEL ACCLAMATION

Alleluia! **Alleluia!**
The Holy Spirit, whom the Father will send in my name, says
the Lord,will teach you everything and remind you of all that
I have said to you. **Alleluia!**

John 14.26

EXTENDED GOSPEL ACCLAMATION

Alleluia! **Alleluia!**
There are varieties of gifts, but the same Spirit.
Alleluia!
There are varieties of service, but the same Lord.
Alleluia!
We were all brought into one body
by baptism in the one Spirit.
Alleluia! [Jesus is Lord!]

1 Corinthians 12.4, 5, 13, 3*

PRAYER AT THE PREPARATION OF THE TABLE

O God, life-giving Spirit,
Spirit of healing and comfort, of integrity and truth,
warm-winged Spirit, brooding over creation,
rushing wind and pentecostal fire,
help us by this sacrament
to commit ourselves to work with you and renew our world;
we ask this in Christ's name.

ADK

COMMUNION SENTENCE

Let those who have been enlightened
and tasted the heavenly gift and shared in the Holy Spirit,
go on towards perfection, alleluia!

cf Hebrews 6.4, 1*

or

By this we know that we abide in God and he in us,
because he has given us of his Spirit, alleluia!

1 John 4.13

_____ Ordinary Time_____

PENTECOST WEEK
Monday to Saturday

INTRODUCTORY SENTENCE

You will be my witnesses, says the Lord, in Jerusalem,
in all Judea and Samaria and to the ends of the earth.

Acts 1.8

GOSPEL ACCLAMATION
Alleluia! **Alleluia!**
Your word is a lantern to my feet and a light upon my path.
Alleluia!

Psalm 119.105

PRAYER AT THE PREPARATION OF THE TABLE

Almighty God,
we pray you to cleanse and defend your Church
and to unite us all in a common bond of love and service;
that we may show forth your goodness and reveal your glory;
through Jesus Christ our Lord.

MSB

COMMUNION SENTENCE

Each of us was given grace according to the measure of
Christ's gift, for building up the body of Christ, until all of us
come to maturity, to the measure of the full stature of Christ.

Ephesians 4.7, 12–13

TRINITY SUNDAY

INTRODUCTORY SENTENCE

Holy, holy, holy is the Lord of hosts;
the whole earth is full of his glory.

Isaiah 6.3

or

Blessed be the Holy Trinity
and blessed be the undivided Unity;
we give thanks for all his loving-kindness towards us.

Traditional

GOSPEL ACCLAMATION

Alleluia! **Alleluia!**
When the Advocate comes, whom I will send to you from the
Father, the Spirit of truth who comes from the Father, he will
testify on my behalf. **Alleluia!**

John 15.26

EXTENDED GOSPEL ACCLAMATION

Alleluia! **Alleluia!**
Blessed be God the Father of mercies
and the God of all consolation;
Alleluia!
Blessed be Jesus Christ, the Son of the living God;
Alleluia!
Blessed be the Holy Spirit
whom God has given to those who obey him;
Alleluia!
[Blessed be the one God, Father, Son and Holy Spirit!]

JPY based on 2 Corinthians 1.3; Matthew 16.16; Acts 5.32

or

Alleluia! **Alleluia!**
Glory to God the Father, maker of all things!
Alleluia!
Glory to his Son Jesus Christ, redeemer of the world!
Alleluia!

Glory to the Holy Spirit, the Lord, the giver of life!
Alleluia!
[Glory to the one God, Father, Son and Holy Spirit!]

JPY

PRAYER AT THE PREPARATION OF THE TABLE

Come, Father of the poor;
come, Light of our hearts,
come, generous Spirit,
by the glory of your creation around us,
by the comfort of your forgiveness within us,
by the wind of your Spirit, renew us,
so that we come glad to this celebration;
through Christ our Lord.

ICWB

COMMUNION SENTENCE

Through Christ we have access in one Spirit to the Father.

Ephesians 2.18*

or

You have been chosen and destined by God the Father
and sanctified by the Spirit to be obedient to Jesus Christ
and to be sprinkled with his blood.

1 Peter 1.2

CORPUS CHRISTI
Day of Thanksgiving for the Holy Communion
Thursday after Trinity Sunday

INTRODUCTORY SENTENCE

The Lord fed his people with the finest wheat, alleluia!
and with honey from the stony rock
   their hunger was satisfied, alleluia, alleluia!

cf Psalm 81.16

GOSPEL ACCLAMATION

Alleluia! **Alleluia!**
Those who eat my flesh and drink my blood have eternal life,
says the Lord, and I will raise them up on the last day.
Alleluia!

John 6.54

PRAYER AT THE PREPARATION OF THE TABLE

Father, your Son gave his disciples a sign
by which to remember him until he comes again:
as bread is broken and wine poured out
may our eyes be opened to know him,
our Lord and Saviour Jesus Christ.

NZPB

COMMUNION SENTENCE

This is the bread that came down from heaven;
the one who eats this bread will live for ever [alleluia!].

John 6.58

SUNDAYS AFTER TRINITY

*After Trinity Sunday the prayers and sentences of the Sundays
after Trinity are used in order (see pages 69–85).*

*If the date of the consecration or dedication of a church is
unknown, the Dedication Festival may be kept on the first Sunday
in October or the Last Sunday after Trinity.*

*On Sundays after Trinity the lectionary provision for Propers 3 to
25 is followed according to calendar date, those of Propers 3 to 7
being used only as necessary from the First Sunday after Trinity.
Proper 3 cannot occur at this point in any year when it has been
used on the Third Sunday before Lent.*

*The Sunday nearest 26 October is always the Last after Trinity
(see pages 83–6). Instead of the material for Proper 25 the
provision for Bible Sunday may be used.*

*The following gospel acclamations are provided for Propers 3 to
24.*

PROPER 3, Sunday nearest 25 May

GOSPEL ACCLAMATION A

Alleluia! **Alleluia!**
You shall be holy, for I the Lord your God am holy. **Alleluia!**
Leviticus 19.2

GOSPEL ACCLAMATION B

Alleluia! **Alleluia!**
Jesus went to Capernaum
and they were astounded at his teaching,
for he taught them as one having authority. **Alleluia!**
Mark 1.21–22

GOSPEL ACCLAMATION C

Alleluia! **Alleluia!**
Do not repay evil for evil or abuse for abuse;
but, on the contrary, repay with a blessing. **Alleluia!**
1 Peter 3.9

PROPER 4, Sunday nearest 1 June

GOSPEL ACCLAMATION A

Alleluia! **Alleluia!**
All authority in heaven and on earth has been given to me,
    says the Lord.
Go therefore and make disciples of all the nations. **Alleluia!**
Matthew 28.18–19

GOSPEL ACCLAMATION B

Alleluia! **Alleluia!**
Observe the sabbath day and keep it holy,
as the Lord your God commanded you. **Alleluia!**
Deuteronomy 5.12

GOSPEL ACCLAMATION C

Alleluia! **Alleluia!**
The gospel is the power of God for salvation to everyone
who has faith, both Jew and Gentile. **Alleluia!**

Romans 1.16*

PROPER 5, Sunday nearest 8 June

GOSPEL ACCLAMATION A

Alleluia! **Alleluia!**
The Lord took our infirmities and bore our diseases.
Alleluia!

Matthew 8.17

GOSPEL ACCLAMATION B

Alleluia! **Alleluia!**
If it is by the Spirit of God I cast out demons, says the Lord,
then the kingdom of God has come to you. **Alleluia!**

Matthew 12.28

GOSPEL ACCLAMATION C

Alleluia! **Alleluia!**
A report about Jesus spread through all the surrounding
country. **Alleluia!**

Luke 4.14

PROPER 6, Sunday nearest 15 June

GOSPEL ACCLAMATION A

Alleluia! **Alleluia!**
It is enough for the disciple to be like the teacher
and the servant like the master, says the Lord. **Alleluia!**

Matthew 10.25*

GOSPEL ACCLAMATION B

Alleluia! **Alleluia!**
To you has been given the mystery of the kingdom of God,
but for those outside, everything comes in parables. **Alleluia!**

Mark 4.11

GOSPEL ACCLAMATION C

Alleluia! **Alleluia!**
I have come to call not the righteous, says the Lord,
but sinners to repentance. **Alleluia!**

Luke 5.32

PROPER 7, Sunday nearest 22 June

GOSPEL ACCLAMATION A

Alleluia! **Alleluia!**
As you go, proclaim the good news:
The kingdom of heaven has come near. **Alleluia!**

Matthew 10.7

GOSPEL ACCLAMATION B

Alleluia! **Alleluia!**
They cried to the Lord in their trouble and he delivered
them from their distress; he stilled the storm to a silence
and quieted the waves of the sea. **Alleluia!**

Psalm 107.28–29

GOSPEL ACCLAMATION C

Alleluia! **Alleluia!**
With authority and power the Lord commands the unclean
spirits and out they come! **Alleluia!**

Luke 4.36

PROPER 8, Sunday nearest 29 June

GOSPEL ACCLAMATION A

Alleluia! **Alleluia!**
What you are to say will be given to you, says the Lord,
for it is not you who speak,
but the Spirit of your Father speaking through you. **Alleluia!**

Matthew 10.19–20

GOSPEL ACCLAMATION B

Alleluia! **Alleluia!**
They begged Jesus that the sick might touch even the fringe
of his cloak and all who touched it were healed. **Alleluia!**

Mark 6.56

GOSPEL ACCLAMATION C

Alleluia! **Alleluia!**
Jesus went through one town and village after another,
teaching as he made his way to Jerusalem. **Alleluia!**

Luke 13.22

PROPER 9, Sunday nearest 6 July

GOSPEL ACCLAMATION A

Alleluia! **Alleluia!**
All the prophets and the law prophesied until John came;
and he is the Elijah who is to come;
let anyone with ears listen! **Alleluia!**

Matthew 11.13–15

GOSPEL ACCLAMATION B

Alleluia! **Alleluia!**
Jesus appointed twelve to be with him
and to be sent out to proclaim the message
and to have authority to cast out demons. **Alleluia!**

Mark 3.14–15

GOSPEL ACCLAMATION C

Alleluia! **Alleluia!**
Anyone who welcomes me, says the Lord,
welcomes the one who sent me. **Alleluia!**

Luke 9.48

PROPER 10, Sunday nearest 13 July

GOSPEL ACCLAMATION A

Alleluia! **Alleluia!**
Blessed are your eyes, for they see, says the Lord,
and your ears, for they hear. **Alleluia!**

Matthew 13.16

GOSPEL ACCLAMATION B

Alleluia! **Alleluia!**
Who do people say that I am, said Jesus,
and who do you say that I am? **Alleluia!**

Mark 8.27, 29

GOSPEL ACCLAMATION C

Alleluia! **Alleluia!**
Assist your neighbour to the best of your ability. **Alleluia!**

Sirach 29.20

PROPER 11, Sunday nearest 20 July

GOSPEL ACCLAMATION A

Alleluia! **Alleluia!**
I will open my mouth in a parable; I will declare the
mysteries of ancient times. **Alleluia!**

Psalm 78.2

GOSPEL ACCLAMATION B

Alleluia! **Alleluia!**
When there was a great crowd Jesus called his disciples
and said to them, I have compassion for the crowd. **Alleluia!**

Mark 8.1–2

GOSPEL ACCLAMATION C

Alleluia! **Alleluia!**
I say this for your own benefit,
to promote unhindered devotion to the Lord. **Alleluia!**

1 Corinthians 7.35

PROPER 12, Sunday nearest 27 July

GOSPEL ACCLAMATION A

Alleluia! **Alleluia!**
The one who sows the good seed is the Son of Man;
the field is the world
and the good seed are the children of the kingdom. **Alleluia!**

Matthew 13.37–38

GOSPEL ACCLAMATION B

Alleluia! **Alleluia!**
Whoever comes to me will never be hungry, says the Lord,
and whoever believes in me will never be thirsty. **Alleluia!**

John 6.35

GOSPEL ACCLAMATION C

Alleluia! **Alleluia!**
If in my name you ask for anything, says the Lord,
I will do it. **Alleluia!**

John 14.14

PROPER 13, Sunday nearest 3 August

GOSPEL ACCLAMATION A

Alleluia! **Alleluia!**
Blessed are those who hunger and thirst for righteousness;
for they will be filled. **Alleluia!**

Matthew 5.6

GOSPEL ACCLAMATION B

Alleluia! **Alleluia!**
I am the living bread from heaven, says the Lord;
whoever eats of this bread will live for ever. **Alleluia!**

John 6.51

GOSPEL ACCLAMATION C

Alleluia! **Alleluia!**
Do not worry about tomorrow;
for tomorrow will bring worries of its own. **Alleluia!**

Matthew 6.34

PROPER 14, Sunday nearest 10 August

GOSPEL ACCLAMATION A

Alleluia! **Alleluia!**
They cried to the Lord in their trouble and he delivered them
from their distress; he stilled the storm to a silence
and quieted the waves of the sea. **Alleluia!**

Psalm 107.28–29

GOSPEL ACCLAMATION B

Alleluia! **Alleluia!**
Do not work for the food which perishes, but for food that
endures for eternal life. **Alleluia!**

John 6.27

GOSPEL ACCLAMATION C

Alleluia! **Alleluia!**
Who is greater, says the Lord,
the one who is at the table or the one who serves?
But I am among you as one who serves. **Alleluia!**

Luke 22.27

PROPER 15, Sunday nearest 17 August

GOSPEL ACCLAMATION A

Alleluia! **Alleluia!**
Go to the lost sheep of the house of Israel
and as you go proclaim the good news,
'The kingdom of heaven has come near.' **Alleluia!**

Matthew 10.6

GOSPEL ACCLAMATION B

Alleluia! **Alleluia!**
The bread of God is he who comes down from heaven
and gives life to the world. **Alleluia!**

John 6.33

GOSPEL ACCLAMATION C

Alleluia! **Alleluia!**
You will be hated by all because of my name, says the Lord;
but the one who endures to the end will be saved. **Alleluia!**

Matthew 10.22; Mark 13.13

PROPER 16, Sunday nearest 24 August

GOSPEL ACCLAMATION A

Alleluia! **Alleluia!**
Truly, Jesus is the Son of God. **Alleluia!**

Matthew 14.33*

GOSPEL ACCLAMATION B

Alleluia! **Alleluia!**
All who see the Son and believe in him will have eternal life,
says the Lord, and I will raise them up on the last day.
Alleluia!

John 6.40*

GOSPEL ACCLAMATION C

Alleluia! **Alleluia!**
The Son of Man is lord of the sabbath. **Alleluia!**

Luke 6.5

PROPER 17, Sunday nearest 31 August

GOSPEL ACCLAMATION A

Alleluia! **Alleluia!**
Whoever does not take up the cross and follow me
is not worthy of me, says the Lord. **Alleluia!**

Matthew 10.38

GOSPEL ACCLAMATION B

Alleluia! **Alleluia!**
To the pure all things are pure. **Alleluia!**

Titus 1.15

GOSPEL ACCLAMATION C

Alleluia! **Alleluia!**
The least among all of you is the greatest, says the Lord.
Alleluia!

Luke 9.48

PROPER 18, Sunday nearest 7 September

GOSPEL ACCLAMATION A

Alleluia! **Alleluia!**
If you abide in me and my words abide in you, says the Lord,
ask for whatever you wish and it will be done for you.
Alleluia!

John 15.7

GOSPEL ACCLAMATION B

Alleluia! **Alleluia!**
Jesus cast out many demons,
but would not permit the demons to speak,
because they knew him. **Alleluia!**

Mark 1.34

GOSPEL ACCLAMATION C

Alleluia! **Alleluia!**
Someone who comes to me, hears my words
and acts on them, says the Lord,
is like a man building a house,
who laid the foundation on rock. **Alleluia!**

Luke 6.47–48

PROPER 19, Sunday nearest 14 September

GOSPEL ACCLAMATION A

Alleluia! **Alleluia!**
Forgive us our debts, as we also have forgiven our debtors.
Alleluia!

Matthew 6.12

GOSPEL ACCLAMATION B

Alleluia! **Alleluia!**
The Son of Man is to be betrayed into human hands
and they will kill him;
and after three days he will rise again. **Alleluia!**

Mark 9.31*

GOSPEL ACCLAMATION C

Alleluia! **Alleluia!**
The Son of Man came to seek out and to save the lost.
Alleluia!

Luke 19.10

PROPER 20, Sunday nearest 21 September

GOSPEL ACCLAMATION A

Alleluia! **Alleluia!**
Many who are first will be last, says the Lord,
and the last will be first. **Alleluia!**

Matthew 19.30

GOSPEL ACCLAMATION B

Alleluia! **Alleluia!**
Let the little children to come to me, says the Lord, for it is to
such as these that the kingdom of God belongs. **Alleluia!**

Mark 10.14

GOSPEL ACCLAMATION C

Alleluia! **Alleluia!**
Lay up your treasure according to the commandments of the
Most High, and it will profit you more than gold. **Alleluia!**

Sirach 29.11

PROPER 21, Sunday nearest 28 September

GOSPEL ACCLAMATION A

Alleluia! **Alleluia!**
The crowds were astounded at his teaching,
for he taught them as one having authority. **Alleluia!**

Matthew 7.28–29

GOSPEL ACCLAMATION B

Alleluia! **Alleluia!**
No one can say, Jesus is Lord, except by the Holy Spirit.
Alleluia!

1 Corinthians 12.3

GOSPEL ACCLAMATION C

Alleluia! **Alleluia!**
The Lord has filled the hungry with good things
and sent the rich away empty. **Alleluia!**

Luke 1.53

PROPER 22, Sunday nearest 5 October

GOSPEL ACCLAMATION A

Alleluia! **Alleluia!**
Come to Christ, a living stone, though rejected by mortals,
yet chosen and precious in God's sight. **Alleluia!**

1 Peter 2.4

GOSPEL ACCLAMATION B

Alleluia! **Alleluia!**
Whoever welcomes one such child in my name
   welcomes me, says the Lord. **Alleluia!**

Mark 9.37

GOSPEL ACCLAMATION C

Alleluia! **Alleluia!**
The greatest among you must become as the youngest,
says the Lord, and the leader like one who serves. **Alleluia!**

Luke 22.26

PROPER 23, Sunday nearest 12 October

GOSPEL ACCLAMATION A

Alleluia! **Alleluia!**
Those who were ready went with the bridegroom into the
wedding banquet. **Alleluia!**

Matthew 25.10

GOSPEL ACCLAMATION B

Alleluia! **Alleluia!**
God has chosen the poor in the world to be rich in faith
and to be heirs of the kingdom that he has promised
to those who love him. **Alleluia!**

James 2.5*

GOSPEL ACCLAMATION C

Alleluia! **Alleluia!**
Go and tell what you have seen and heard:
the lepers are cleansed and the poor have good news
brought to them. **Alleluia!**

Luke 7.22

or

Alleluia! **Alleluia!**
You have already been cleansed, says the Lord,
by the word that I have spoken to you. **Alleluia!**

John 15.3

PROPER 24, Sunday nearest 19 October

GOSPEL ACCLAMATION A

Alleluia! **Alleluia!**
I urge that prayers should be made for all who are in high
positions; this is right and is acceptable in the sight of God
our Saviour. **Alleluia!**

1 Timothy 2.1–3

GOSPEL ACCLAMATION B

Alleluia! **Alleluia!**
The greater you are, the more you must humble yourself;
so you will find favour in the sight of the Lord. **Alleluia!**

Sirach 3.18

or

Alleluia! **Alleluia!**
Humble yourselves before the Lord and he will exalt you.
Alleluia!

James 4.10

GOSPEL ACCLAMATION C

Alleluia! **Alleluia!**
Ask and it will be given to you; search and you will find.
Alleluia!

Luke 11.9

PROPER 25, Sunday nearest 26 October, Last after Trinity

See pages 83–6.

—

THE FIRST SUNDAY AFTER TRINITY

INTRODUCTORY SENTENCE

You are the God of the lowly, the helper of the oppressed,
upholder of the weak, protector of the forsaken,
saviour of those without hope.

Judith 9.11

or

The Lord is my strength and my shield;
my heart trusts in him
and I am helped.

Psalm 28.7

PRAYER AT THE PREPARATION OF THE TABLE

Eternal God, your word inspires our faith:
may we who offer you our praise trust you in all things;
we ask this in the name of Jesus Christ our Lord.

BAS

COMMUNION SENTENCE

Faith is the assurance of things hoped for,
the conviction of things not seen.

Hebrews 11.1

—

THE SECOND SUNDAY AFTER TRINITY

INTRODUCTORY SENTENCE

In this is love, not that we loved God but that he loved us
and sent his Son to be the atoning sacrifice for our sins.

1 John 4.10

PRAYER AT THE PREPARATION OF THE TABLE

Generous and faithful God,
grant that by the grace of this sacrament
our lives may bring forth the fruit of the Spirit
   in love and joy and peace;
we ask this through Christ our Lord.

JPY

COMMUNION SENTENCE

The kingdom of God is righteousness and peace
and joy in the Holy Spirit.

Romans 14.17

THE THIRD SUNDAY AFTER TRINITY

INTRODUCTORY SENTENCE

You did not receive a spirit of slavery to fall back into fear,
but you have received a spirit of adoption, by which we cry,
'Abba, Father'.

Romans 8.15–16*

PRAYER AT THE PREPARATION OF THE TABLE

Heavenly Father,
we bring before you these gifts of your own creation
and we offer the service of our lives
   to the praise and glory of your name;
through your Son Jesus Christ our Lord.

JPY

COMMUNION SENTENCE

One thing have I asked of the Lord, one thing I seek;
that I may dwell in the house of the Lord
all the days of my life.

Psalm 27.4

or

We have waited in silence on your loving kindness, O God,
in the midst of your temple.

Psalm 48.9

———

THE FOURTH SUNDAY AFTER TRINITY

INTRODUCTORY SENTENCE

We look not at what can be seen but at what cannot be seen;
for what can be seen is temporary,
but what cannot be seen is eternal.

2 Corinthians 4.18

PRAYER AT THE PREPARATION OF THE TABLE

Lord Jesus Christ,
you came to live among us in time and in space,
grant that in this holy feast
   we may live in your eternal kingdom;
who are alive and reign, now and for ever.

JPY

COMMUNION SENTENCE

The Lord rebuilds Jerusalem;
he gathers the exiles of Israel;
he heals the broken-hearted and binds up their wounds.

Psalm 147.2–3

———

71

THE FIFTH SUNDAY AFTER TRINITY

INTRODUCTORY SENTENCE

Clothe yourselves with the new self, created according to the likeness of God in true righteousness and holiness.

Ephesians 4.24

PRAYER AT THE PREPARATION OF THE TABLE

Father,
your word creates in us a yearning for your kingdom:
fulfill our longing and keep us in your peace;
for the sake of Jesus Christ our Lord.

BAS*

COMMUNION SENTENCE

I urge that supplications, prayers, intercessions
and thanksgivings should be made for everyone,
so that we may lead a quiet and peaceable life
in all godliness and dignity.

1 Timothy 2.1–2

or

God governs the peoples; he gives food in abundance.

Job 36.31

THE SIXTH SUNDAY AFTER TRINITY

INTRODUCTORY SENTENCE

In everything by prayer and supplication with thanksgiving
let your requests be made known to God. And the peace of
God, which surpasses all understanding, will guard your
hearts and your minds in Christ Jesus.

Philippians 4.6–7

or

God has chosen the poor in the world to be rich in faith and to be heirs of the kingdom that he has promised to those who love him.

James 2.5

PRAYER AT THE PREPARATION OF THE TABLE

God of grace,
as we look forward to the glory you have promised,
fulfil our hopes and transform our lives;
through Jesus Christ our Lord.

BAS*

COMMUNION SENTENCE

The Lord leads me beside still waters; he revives my soul;
and guides me along right pathways for his name's sake.

Psalm 23.2–3

THE SEVENTH SUNDAY AFTER TRINITY

INTRODUCTORY SENTENCE

Turn to me in mercy,
as you always do to those who love your name.

Psalm 119.132

PRAYER AT THE PREPARATION OF THE TABLE

Lord Jesus Christ, by the grace of this sacrament,
keep us grafted into you, the living vine;
and grant that always abiding in you
    we may bear fruit to your glory;
who are alive and reign, now and for ever.

JPY

COMMUNION SENTENCE

I am the vine, you are the branches, says the Lord.
Abide in me, as I abide in you.

John 15.5, 4

THE EIGHTH SUNDAY AFTER TRINITY

INTRODUCTORY SENTENCE

All who take refuge in you will be glad;
they will sing out their joy for ever; you will shelter them,
so that those who love your name may exult in you.

Psalm 5.11

PRAYER AT THE PREPARATION OF THE TABLE

Lord Jesus Christ, according to your command
we bring these gifts of bread and wine:
grant that your precious body and blood
may keep our souls and bodies in your eternal life;
who are alive and reign, now and for ever.

JPY

COMMUNION SENTENCE

What was from the beginning, what we have heard, what we
have seen with our eyes, what we have looked at and
touched with our hands, concerning the word of life, we
declare to you, so that your joy may be complete.

1 John 1.1, 4

THE NINTH SUNDAY AFTER TRINITY

INTRODUCTORY SENTENCE

The fruit of the Spirit is love, joy, peace, patience, kindness,
generosity, faithfulness, gentleness and self-control.
If we live by the Spirit, let us also be guided by the Spirit.

Galatians 5.22–23, 25

PRAYER AT THE PREPARATION OF THE TABLE

Lord Jesus Christ,
may our hearts be open to your love,
our doors to friend and stranger,
our table to all whom you call to your supper,
and our lives to your risen life;
who are alive and reign, now and for ever.

JPY

COMMUNION SENTENCE

If you hear my voice and open the door, says the Lord,
I will come in to you and eat with you and you with me.

Revelation 3.20

THE TENTH SUNDAY AFTER TRINITY

INTRODUCTORY SENTENCE

Lord, hear my prayer
and in your faithfulness heed my supplications;
answer me in your righteousness.

Psalm 143.1

PRAYER AT THE PREPARATION OF THE TABLE

O Lord, our strength and our song,
open to us the gates of righteousness,
that we may enter through them and give you thanks;

may we know your light and your salvation
and receive the blessings of your house;
whose steadfast loves endures for ever and ever.

JPY based on Psalm 118

COMMUNION SENTENCE

I am the gate, says the Lord;
whoever enters by me will be saved
and will come in and go out and find food.

John 10.9*

THE ELEVENTH SUNDAY AFTER TRINITY

INTRODUCTORY SENTENCE

The Lord waits to be gracious to you;
he will rise up to show mercy to you;
for the Lord is a God of justice;
blessed are all those who wait for him.

Isaiah 30.18

PRAYER AT THE PREPARATION OF THE TABLE

Almighty and most merciful God,
out of the fullness of your gifts we bring before you
this bread and wine, [our money] and our lives.
Blessed be your holy name for ever;
through Jesus Christ our Lord.

URSB

COMMUNION SENTENCE

By God's will we have been sanctified
through the offering of the body of Jesus Christ once for all.

Hebrews 10.10

THE TWELFTH SUNDAY AFTER TRINITY

INTRODUCTORY SENTENCE

Let not your hearts be troubled, says the Lord.
I will ask the Father and he will give you another Helper,
to be with you for ever.

John 14.1, 16

PRAYER AT THE PREPARATION OF THE TABLE

God of life and health,
in your Son Jesus Christ we find forgiveness of all that is past:
grant that in this eucharist today we may find the healing of
   all our sins;
 we ask this in the name of Jesus Christ our Lord.

BAS

COMMUNION SENTENCE

The Lord will give healing for your flesh and refreshment for
your body.

Proverbs 3.8*

THE THIRTEENTH SUNDAY AFTER TRINITY

INTRODUCTORY SENTENCE

God reconciled us to himself through Christ
and has given us the ministry of reconciliation.

2 Corinthians 5.18

PRAYER AT THE PREPARATION OF THE TABLE

Living host, call us together,
call us to eat and drink with you;
grant that by your body and your blood
we may be drawn to each other and to you;
who are alive and reign, now and for ever.

NZPB

COMMUNION SENTENCE

The bread of God is he who comes down from heaven
and gives life to the world, says the Lord;
whoever comes to me will never be hungry
and whoever believes in me will never be thirsty.

John 6.33, 35

THE FOURTEENTH SUNDAY
AFTER TRINITY

INTRODUCTORY SENTENCE

We have confidence to enter the sanctuary by the blood of
Jesus, by the new and living way that he has opened for us.

Hebrews 10.19–20

or

God is spirit and those who worship him must worship in
spirit and in truth.

John 4.24

PRAYER AT THE PREPARATION OF THE TABLE

Great and holy God, accept our offering of labour and love:
may we bring you true and spiritual worship
and be one with you through Jesus Christ our Lord.

BAS

COMMUNION SENTENCE

Remember, I am with you always,
to the end of the age, says the Lord.

Matthew 28.20

THE FIFTEENTH SUNDAY
AFTER TRINITY

INTRODUCTORY SENTENCE

Stand firm in your faith and let all that you do be done in love.
1 Corinthians 16.13–14

PRAYER AT THE PREPARATION OF THE TABLE

Lord Jesus Christ, you have opened the scriptures to us:
let our hearts burn with your love,
be known to us in the breaking of the bread,
and abide with us always that we may abide in you;
who live and reign now and for ever.

JPY

COMMUNION SENTENCE

Those who abide in me and I in them bear much fruit,
says the Lord, because apart from me you can do nothing.
John 15.5

THE SIXTEENTH SUNDAY
AFTER TRINITY

INTRODUCTORY SENTENCE

Answer me when I call, O God, defender of my cause;
have mercy on me and hear my prayer.
Psalm 4.1

PRAYER AT THE PREPARATION OF THE TABLE

Merciful God, give us grace to love one another
that your love may be made perfect in us;
we ask this in the name of Jesus Christ our Lord.

BAS*

COMMUNION SENTENCE

The whole law is summed up in a single commandment:
You shall love your neighbour as yourself.

Galatians 5.14

THE SEVENTEENTH SUNDAY
AFTER TRINITY

INTRODUCTORY SENTENCE

Come to me, says the Lord,
and you will find rest for your souls.

Matthew 11.28, 29

PRAYER AT THE PREPARATION OF THE TABLE

Lord,
help us to see what is eternally good and true
and having seen to go on searching
until we come to the joys of heaven;
through Jesus Christ our Lord.

NZPB*

COMMUNION SENTENCE

Let your light shine before others, so that they may see your
good works and give glory to your Father in heaven.

Matthew 5.16

THE EIGHTEENTH SUNDAY AFTER TRINITY

INTRODUCTORY SENTENCE

Teach me, O Lord, the way of your statutes
   and I shall keep it to the end;
I will run the way of your commandments,
   for you have set my heart at liberty.

Psalm 119.33, 32

PRAYER AT THE PREPARATION OF THE TABLE

God of grace, you have freed us from our sins
and made us a kingdom in your Son Jesus Christ our Lord:
deepen our knowledge of your ways
and strengthen us in the new life you have given us;
through Jesus Christ our Lord.

BAS*

COMMUNION SENTENCE

I confer on you a kingdom, says the Lord,
as my Father has conferred on me,
so that you may eat and drink at my table in my kingdom.

Luke 22.29–30

THE NINETEENTH SUNDAY AFTER TRINITY

INTRODUCTORY SENTENCE

Let the peace of Christ rule in your hearts, to which indeed
you were called in the one body; and be thankful.

Colossians 3.15

PRAYER AT THE PREPARATION OF THE TABLE

Eternal God, we come with these gifts
to offer the praise of our lips and the service of our lives;
through Jesus Christ our Lord.

URSB

COMMUNION SENTENCE

Let us love not in word or speech, but in truth and action.

1 John 3.18

THE TWENTIETH SUNDAY
AFTER TRINITY

INTRODUCTORY SENTENCE

Lord, teach me to do what pleases you, for you are my God;
let your good Spirit lead me on level ground.

Psalm 143.10

PRAYER AT THE PREPARATION OF THE TABLE

God of wisdom:
enrich our lives with the gifts of your Spirit,
that we may follow the way of our Lord Jesus Christ
and serve one another in freedom;
we ask this in his name.

BAS*

COMMUNION SENTENCE

I pray that with the eyes of your heart enlightened, you may
know what is the hope to which God has called you, what
are the riches of his glorious inheritance among the saints
and what is the immeasurable greatness of his power.

Ephesians 1.18–19

THE TWENTY-FIRST SUNDAY AFTER TRINITY

INTRODUCTORY SENTENCE

Let us approach the sanctuary with a true heart,
in full assurance of faith,
our hearts sprinkled clean from an evil conscience
and our bodies washed with pure water.

Hebrews 10.22

PRAYER AT THE PREPARATION OF THE TABLE

Universal and unchanging God,
we are one, unalterably one with all the human race:
grant that we who come to share in Christ's body and blood
may by your unifying Spirit
   break down the walls that divide us;
we ask this through the same Christ our Lord.

NZPB*

COMMUNION SENTENCE

If we walk in the light as God himself is in the light,
we have fellowship with one another
and the blood of Jesus his Son cleanses us from all sin.

1 John 1.7

LAST SUNDAY AFTER TRINITY

See also Dedication Festival, pages 85–6.

INTRODUCTORY SENTENCE

Accept, O Lord, the willing tribute of my lips;
and teach me your judgments.

Psalm 119.108

or (especially for Bible Sunday)

83

Whatever was written in former days was written for our instruction, that by steadfastness and the encouragement of the scriptures we might have hope.

Romans 15.4

GOSPEL ACCLAMATION A

Alleluia! **Alleluia!**
If you wish to enter into life, keep the commandments.
Alleluia!

Matthew 19.17

GOSPEL ACCLAMATION B

Alleluia! **Alleluia!**
The Lord opens the eyes of the blind;
the Lord lifts up those who are bowed down;
the Lord loves the righteous. **Alleluia!**

Psalm 146.8

GOSPEL ACCLAMATION C

Alleluia! **Alleluia!**
The Lord has brought down the powerful and lifted up the lowly. **Alleluia!**

Luke 1.52

GOSPEL ACCLAMATION: BIBLE SUNDAY

Alleluia! **Alleluia!**
The word of our God will stand for ever. **Alleluia!**

Isaiah 40.8

or

Alleluia! **Alleluia!**
Heaven and earth will pass away, says the Lord,
but my words will not pass away. **Alleluia!**

Matthew 24.35; Mark 13.31; Luke 21.33

PRAYER AT THE PREPARATION OF THE TABLE

Lord God, you have opened to us the scriptures:
grant that in the breaking of this bread
we may recognize the Word made flesh,
your Son Jesus Christ our Lord.

JPY

COMMUNION SENTENCE

Blessed are you who are hungry now, says the Lord,
for you will be filled.

Luke 6.21

or (for Bible Sunday)

How sweet are your words to my taste,
they are sweeter than honey to my mouth!

Psalm 119.103

DEDICATION FESTIVAL

First Sunday in October or Last Sunday after Trinity

INTRODUCTORY SENTENCE

How awesome is this place!
This is none other than the house of God
    and this is the gate of heaven.

Genesis 28.17

or

How dear to me is your dwelling, O Lord of hosts!
My soul has a desire and longing for the courts of the Lord;
my heart and my flesh rejoice in the living God.

Psalm 84.1–2

GOSPEL ACCLAMATION A

Alleluia! **Alleluia!**
I will make those who keep my covenant joyful in my house
of prayer; for my house shall be called a house of prayer for
all peoples. **Alleluia!**

Isaiah 56.7

GOSPEL ACCLAMATION B

Alleluia! **Alleluia!**
The latter splendour of this house
    shall be greater than the former. **Alleluia!**

Haggai 1.9

GOSPEL ACCLAMATION C

Alleluia! **Alleluia!**
The Lord whom you seek will suddenly come to his temple,
the messenger of the covenant in whom you delight –
indeed he is coming, says the Lord of hosts. **Alleluia!**

Malachi 3.1

PRAYER AT THE PREPARATION OF THE TABLE

Father, you have appointed our Lord Jesus Christ
as mediator of a new covenant:
give us grace to draw near with fullness of faith
and join ourselves in a perpetual covenant with you;
through Jesus Christ our Lord.

MSB

COMMUNION SENTENCE

Be silent before the Lord God,
   for the day of the Lord is at hand;
the Lord has prepared a sacrifice,
   he has consecrated his guests.

Zephaniah 1.7

or

Present your bodies as a living sacrifice,
holy and acceptable to God.

Romans 12.1

ALL SAINTS

1 November or the Fourth Sunday before Advent

INTRODUCTORY SENTENCE

Give thanks to the Father, who has enabled you to share in
the inheritance of the saints in light.

Colossians 1.12

GOSPEL ACCLAMATION

Alleluia! **Alleluia!**
Blessed and holy are those who share in the first resurrection.
[Over these the second death has no power,
but they will be priests of God and of Christ
and they will reign with him for a thousand years.]
Alleluia!

Revelation 20.6

or

Alleluia! **Alleluia!**
Blessed are those who keep the words of this book. **Alleluia!**

Revelation 22.7

or

Alleluia! **Alleluia!**
Blessed are those who wash their robes,
so that they will have the right to the tree of life
and may enter the city by the gates. **Alleluia!**

Revelation 22.14

PRAYER AT THE PREPARATION OF THE TABLE

Holy and mighty God,
we give you thanks for the triumph of Christ
in the lives of all his saints:
help us, like them, to run our course with faith,
that we may come to your eternal kingdom;
through the same Jesus Christ our Lord.

BAS*

COMMUNION SENTENCE

You are no longer strangers and aliens, but you are citizens
with the saints and also members of the household of God.

Ephesians 2.19

THE FOURTH SUNDAY BEFORE ADVENT

For use when All Saints' Day is observed on a weekday.

INTRODUCTORY SENTENCE

With the eyes of your heart enlightened,
may you know the hope to which God has called you,
and the riches of his glorious inheritance among the saints.

Ephesians 1.18

GOSPEL ACCLAMATION A

Alleluia! **Alleluia!**
You will be hated by all because of my name, says the Lord,
but the one who stands firm to the end will be saved.
Alleluia!

Matthew 10.22

GOSPEL ACCLAMATION B

Alleluia! **Alleluia!**
In sacrifice and offering you take no pleasure;
I love to do your will, O my God;
your law is deep in my heart. **Alleluia!**

Psalm 40.6, 8

GOSPEL ACCLAMATION C

Alleluia! **Alleluia!**
I have come to call not the righteous, says the Lord,
but sinners to repentance. **Alleluia!**

Luke 5.32

PRAYER AT THE PREPARATION OF THE TABLE

Lord God almighty,
you surround us with a great cloud of witnesses:
grant that as they now sit and feast in your kingdom,
we may follow them in the way of eternal life;
through Jesus Christ our Lord.

*BCO**

COMMUNION SENTENCE

You have come to Mount Zion
and to the city of the living God, the heavenly Jerusalem
and to the assembly of the firstborn in heaven
and to the spirits of the righteous made perfect.

*Hebrews 12.22–23**

or

May you have the power to comprehend, with all the saints,
what is the breadth and length and height and depth
and to know the love of Christ,
that you may be filled with all the fullness of God.

Ephesians 3.18–19

THE THIRD SUNDAY BEFORE ADVENT

INTRODUCTORY SENTENCE

Christ Jesus came to proclaim peace to you who were far off
and peace to those who were near.

Ephesians 2.17

GOSPEL ACCLAMATION A

Alleluia! **Alleluia!**
Not everyone who says to me, Lord, Lord,
will enter the kingdom of heaven,
but only one who does the will of my Father in heaven.
Alleluia!

Matthew 7.21

89

GOSPEL ACCLAMATION B

Alleluia! **Alleluia!**
Repent, for the kingdom of heaven has come near. **Alleluia!**

Matthew 3.2

GOSPEL ACCLAMATION C

Alleluia! **Alleluia!**
My kingdom is not of this world, says the Lord. **Alleluia!**

John 18.36

PRAYER AT THE PREPARATION OF THE TABLE

Holy God, in Christ you make all things one:
may we who are reconciled at this table
bring wholeness to our broken world;
we ask this in the name of Jesus Christ our Lord.

BAS*

COMMUNION SENTENCE

On either side of the river is the tree of life with its twelve
kinds of fruit, producing its fruit each month; and the leaves
of the tree are for the healing of the nations.

Revelation 22.2

THE SECOND SUNDAY BEFORE ADVENT

INTRODUCTORY SENTENCE

Stand up and raise your heads,
because your redemption is drawing near.

Luke 21.28

GOSPEL ACCLAMATION A

Alleluia! **Alleluia!**
When the Son of Man is seated on the throne of his glory,
you will also sit on twelve thrones, judging the twelve tribes
of Israel. **Alleluia!**

Matthew 19.28

GOSPEL ACCLAMATION B

Alleluia! **Alleluia!**
The good news must first be proclaimed to all nations.
Alleluia!

Mark 13.12

GOSPEL ACCLAMATION C

Alleluia! **Alleluia!**
The good news of the kingdom will be proclaimed
throughout the world, as a testimony to all the nations;
and then the end will come. **Alleluia!**

Matthew 24.14

PRAYER AT THE PREPARATION OF THE TABLE

Father, you call us to be your servants;
fill us with the courage and love of Jesus,
that all the world may gather in joy
    at the table of your kingdom;
we ask this through Christ our Lord.

BAS*

COMMUNION SENTENCE

Set all your hope on the grace that Jesus Christ will bring you
when he is revealed.

1 Peter 1.13

CHRIST THE KING
The Sunday before Advent

INTRODUCTORY SENTENCE

Worthy is the Lamb to receive power and wealth and
wisdom and might and honour and glory and blessing!

Revelation 5.11

GOSPEL ACCLAMATION

Alleluia! **Alleluia!**
Some standing here will not taste death until they see
that the kingdom of God has come with power. **Alleluia!**

Mark 9.1

or

Alleluia! **Alleluia!**
Blessed is the king who comes in the name of the Lord!
Alleluia!

Luke 19.38

PRAYER AT THE PREPARATION OF THE TABLE

Eternal God,
you have given your Son authority in heaven and on earth:
grant that through this eucharist
we may share in the banquet of his kingdom
and serve him with hope and joy;
who is alive and reigns, now and for ever.

NZPB*

COMMUNION SENTENCE

You shall eat and drink at my table in my kingdom, says the
Lord.

Luke 22.30

or

The kingdom of the world has become
the kingdom of our Lord and of his Christ,
and he will reign forever and ever.

Revelation 11.15

Holy Days

Holy Days

Full provision is not made here for most lesser festivals. The provision for the Common of Saints (pages 133–44) may be used, together with the authorized collects and other material from the Calendar, Lectionary and Collects.

THE NAMING AND CIRCUMCISION
OF JESUS
1 January

INTRODUCTORY SENTENCE

I give you thanks, O Lord and King,
and praise you, O God my Saviour.

Sirach 51.1

GOSPEL ACCLAMATION

Alleluia! **Alleluia!**
You will conceive in your womb and bear a son
and you will name him Jesus. **Alleluia!**

Luke 1.31

PRAYER AT THE PREPARATION OF THE TABLE

O Lord our God,
    by the name of Jesus salvation has come to the world:
may our worship and our lives glorify his holy Name,
who is alive and reigns, now and for ever.

JPY

COMMUNION SENTENCE

May the name of our Lord Jesus be glorified in you and you in him, according to the grace of our God and the Lord Jesus Christ.

2 Thessalonians 1.12

THE CONVERSION OF SAINT PAUL
25 January

INTRODUCTORY SENTENCE

I am unfit to be called an apostle,
because I persecuted the Church of God,
but by the grace of God I am what I am.

1 Corinthians 15.9–10

GOSPEL ACCLAMATION

Alleluia! **Alleluia!**
You will be the Lord's witness to all the world of what you
have seen and heard. **Alleluia!**

Acts 22.15

PRAYER AT THE PREPARATION OF THE TABLE

Lord Jesus Christ,
we have heard your apostles' teaching:
keep us united in their fellowship by the breaking of this bread;
we make our prayer in your name.

JPY

or

Almighty God:
as we celebrate this holy eucharist,
may your Spirit fill us with the light of faith;
by the grace of our Lord Jesus Christ.

BAS*

COMMUNION SENTENCE

Paul said, 'I urge you to take food for your salvation.'
Then he took bread and giving thanks to God,
broke it and began to eat;
and they were all encouraged and took food.

Acts 27.34–36*

THE PRESENTATION OF CHRIST
IN THE TEMPLE
(CANDLEMAS)
2 February
or the Sunday nearest 31 January

See pages 18–19.

TIMOTHY AND TITUS
26 January

INTRODUCTORY SENTENCE

As for you, man of God, pursue righteousness, godliness,
faith, love, endurance, gentleness.

1 Timothy 6.11

GOSPEL ACCLAMATION
Alleluia! **Alleluia!**
Proclaim the word and insist upon it; reprove, encourage and
exhort, with all patience in your teaching. **Alleluia!**

2 Timothy 4.2

PRAYER AT THE PREPARATION OF THE TABLE
Loving God,
who bestowed such gifts upon Timothy and Titus
that they rejoiced to offer you their lives:

give us grace to render the gifts of true and
    acceptable worship;
through Jesus Christ our Lord.

*FAS**

COMMUNION SENTENCE

The grace of God has appeared, which brings salvation to all.

Titus 2.11

SAINT JOSEPH OF NAZARETH
19 March

*'Alleluia' is said only when this Feast is transferred to a day in
Eastertide.*

INTRODUCTORY SENTENCE

Joseph was the husband of Mary [alleluia!],
of whom Jesus was born, called the Christ [alleluia, alleluia!].

Matthew 1.16

GOSPEL ACCLAMATION

IN LENT

Praise be to the Lord Jesus!
The child's father and mother were amazed
at what was being said about him.
Praise be to the Lord Jesus!

Luke 2.33

IN EASTERTIDE

Alleluia! **Alleluia!**
The child's father and mother were amazed
at what was being said about him. **Alleluia!**

Luke 2.33

PRAYER AT THE PREPARATION OF THE TABLE

Lord our God,
as Joseph consecrated Jesus to you
and cherished him in his home at Nazareth:
grant that we may always cherish Christ
and that our hearts may be his dwelling place,
now and for ever.

JPY

COMMUNION SENTENCE

When Joseph and Mary had finished
everything required by the law of the Lord,
they returned to their own town of Nazareth [alleluia!].

Luke 2.39

THE ANNUNCIATION OF OUR LORD
25 March

'Alleluia' is omitted when this Feast is observed during Lent.

INTRODUCTORY SENTENCE

I am Gabriel; I stand in the presence of God [alleluia!],
and I have been sent to bring you this good news
    [alleluia, alleluia!].

Luke 1.19

GOSPEL ACCLAMATION

IN LENT

Praise and honour to Christ Jesus!
Blessed is she who believed that there would be a fulfilment
of what was spoken to her by the Lord.
Praise and honour to Christ Jesus!

Luke 1.45

IN EASTERTIDE

Alleluia! **Alleluia!**
Blessed is she who believed that there would be a fulfilment
of what was spoken to her by the Lord. **Alleluia!**

Luke 1.45

EXTENDED ACCLAMATION

BEFORE EASTER

My soul magnifies the Lord:
Holy is his name!
He has looked with favour on his lowly servant:
Holy is his name!
His mercy endures from generation to generation:
Holy is his name!

Luke 1.46–50*

IN EASTERTIDE

Alleluia! **Alleluia!**
Hail, O favoured one, the Lord is with you:
Alleluia!
Behold the handmaid of the Lord:
Alleluia!
The Word became flesh and dwelt among us:
Alleluia!

Luke 1.28, 38*; John 1.14*

PRAYER AT THE PREPARATION OF THE TABLE

Heavenly Father,
as your Son came into the world, taking our human nature,
grant that in this sacrament
he may make known among us his divine glory;
who is alive and reigns, now and for ever.

JPY

COMMUNION SENTENCE

The young woman is with child and shall bear a son
and shall name him Immanuel [alleluia!].

Isaiah 7.14

or

The Word became flesh and lived among us [alleluia!].

John 1.14

SAINT GEORGE THE MARTYR
23 April

INTRODUCTORY SENTENCE

Take up the whole armour of God, alleluia!
so that you may be able to withstand on that evil day
and having done everything, to stand firm, alleluia, alleluia!

Ephesians 6.13

or

Our brothers have conquered their accuser by the blood of
the Lamb
and by the word of their testimony, alleluia!
for they did not cling to life even in the face of death,
alleluia, alleluia!

Revelation 12.11

GOSPEL ACCLAMATION

Alleluia! **Alleluia!**
You will be hated by all because of my name,
but the one who endures to the end will be saved. **Alleluia!**

Matthew 10.22

PRAYER AT THE PREPARATION OF THE TABLE

Lord Jesus Christ,
through this sacrament
we know your death to be the way to life eternal:

grant that we who celebrate the faithfulness
of your martyr George, even to death,
may share with him the victory of your risen life;
who are alive and reign, now and for ever.

JPY

COMMUNION SENTENCE

To everyone who conquers I will give permission to eat from
the tree of life, which is in the paradise of God, alleluia!

Revelation 2.7

SAINT MARK THE EVANGELIST
25 April

INTRODUCTORY SENTENCE

The disciples went out and
    proclaimed the good news everywhere, alleluia!
while the Lord worked with them and confirmed the word
    with the signs that accompanied it, alleluia, alleluia!

Mark 16.20

or

The word of the Lord continued to advance, alleluia!
and John, whose other name was Mark,
    came from Jerusalem with the apostles, alleluia, alleluia!

Acts 12.24–25*

GOSPEL ACCLAMATION

Alleluia! **Alleluia!**
The good news must be proclaimed to all nations. **Alleluia!**

Mark 13.10

PRAYER AT THE PREPARATION OF THE TABLE

Almighty God,
we have heard the good news of eternal salvation:
grant that we may follow your servant Mark
in the household of faith and in the ministry of the gospel;
through your Son Jesus Christ our Lord.

JPY

COMMUNION SENTENCE

Go into the world and proclaim the gospel
  to the whole creation, alleluia!

Mark 16.15

SAINT PHILIP AND SAINT JAMES
THE APOSTLES
1 May

INTRODUCTORY SENTENCE

Can anything good come out of Nazareth? alleluia!
Come and see, alleluia, alleluia!

John 1.46

GOSPEL ACCLAMATION

Alleluia! **Alleluia!**
Some of those who went up to worship at the festival
said to Philip, Sir, we wish to see Jesus. **Alleluia!**

John 12.21*

or

Alleluia! **Alleluia!**
You will know that I am in my Father, says the Lord,
and you in me and I in you. **Alleluia!**

John 14.20

103

PRAYER AT THE PREPARATION OF THE TABLE

Father, your Son Jesus Christ calls us,
and we desire both to see and to follow him:
grant that in this sacred feast
we may be fed with the bread which is beyond price,
your Son Jesus Christ our Lord.

JPY

COMMUNION SENTENCE

Whoever has seen me has seen the Father, says the Lord,
alleluia!

John 14.9

ENGLISH SAINTS AND MARTYRS OF THE REFORMATION ERA
4 May

INTRODUCTORY SENTENCE

These are they who have come out of the great ordeal, alleluia!
they have washed their robes and made them white
   in the blood of the Lamb, alleluia, alleluia!

Revelation 7.14

GOSPEL ACCLAMATION

Alleluia! **Alleluia!**
Many will fall away and they will betray one another and
hate one another; the love of many will grow cold, but
anyone who endures to the end will be saved. **Alleluia!**

Matthew 24.10–13

PRAYER AT THE PREPARATION OF THE TABLE

Lord Jesus Christ, in this world we have tribulation:
through this sacrament grant us that peace
   which the world cannot give;
that we may know that you have overcome the world;
and that you live and reign, now and for ever.

JPY

or

God of mercy and forgiveness:
grant that in contending for your truth
we may have grace to put on the righteousness of Christ,
and worship you by faith with thanksgiving;
through Jesus Christ our Lord.

FAS

COMMUNION SENTENCE

You will be betrayed even by parents and brothers, relatives
and friends; and they will put some of you to death;
but by your endurance you will gain your souls, alleluia!

Luke 21.16, 19

SAINT MATTHIAS THE APOSTLE
14 May

*'Alleluia' is omitted from the introductory and communion
sentences when this Feast is observed after Pentecost.*

INTRODUCTORY SENTENCE

I choose to give the last-comer a generous reward [alleluia!],
so the last will be first and the first last, says the Lord
   [alleluia, alleluia!].

Matthew 20.14–16*

or

The kingdom of God will be taken away
and given to a people that produces the fruits of the kingdom
[alleluia, alleluia!].

Matthew 21.41

GOSPEL ACCLAMATION

Alleluia! **Alleluia!**
You are to testify on my behalf, says the Lord,
because you have been with me from the beginning.
Alleluia!

John 15.27

PRAYER AT THE PREPARATION OF THE TABLE

Lord, your banquet is ready:
call us from streets and alleys,
from highways and hedges,
from east and west, from north and south,
to a place at the feast in your kingdom,
where you are alive and reign, now and for ever.

JPY

COMMUNION SENTENCE

Blessed are those servants
whom the master finds alert when he comes;
he will have them sit down to eat
and he will come and serve them, [alleluia!]

Luke 12.37

THE VISIT OF THE BLESSED VIRGIN MARY TO ELIZABETH
31 May

*'Alleluia' is omitted from the introductory and communion
sentences when this Feast is observed after Pentecost.*

INTRODUCTORY SENTENCE

My heart exults in the Lord [alleluia!],
my strength is exalted in my God [alleluia, alleluia!].

1 Samuel 2.1

GOSPEL ACCLAMATION

Alleluia! **Alleluia!**
The Lord makes the woman of a childless house
to be a joyful mother of children. **Alleluia!**

Psalm 113.9

or

Alleluia! **Alleluia!**
Here I am, the servant of the Lord;
let it be with me according to your word. **Alleluia!**

Luke 1.38

PRAYER AT THE PREPARATION OF THE TABLE

God of the humble and expectant,
you bless those who believe when you promise:
help us, like Mary and Elizabeth,
simply to delight in the good things you prepare for us;
we ask this through Christ our Lord.

NZPB*

COMMUNION SENTENCE

The Lord has filled the hungry with good things [alleluia!].

Luke 1.53

SAINT BARNABAS THE APOSTLE
11 June

*'Alleluia' is omitted from the introductory and communion
sentences when this Feast is observed after Pentecost.*

INTRODUCTORY SENTENCE

I have set you to be a light for the nations [alleluia!],
so that you may bring salvation to the ends of the earth
[alleluia, alleluia!].

Acts 13.47

GOSPEL ACCLAMATION

Alleluia! **Alleluia!**
We bring you good news that you should turn to the living
God, who made the heaven and the earth and the sea and all
that is in them. **Alleluia!**

Acts 14.15

PRAYER AT THE PREPARATION OF THE TABLE

Living God,
whose servant Barnabas brought relief to those in need
and encouragement to the faint-hearted,
by this sacrament satisfy our hunger and strengthen our hearts;
through Jesus Christ our Lord.

JPY

COMMUNION SENTENCE

The living God fills you with food and your hearts with joy
[alleluia!].

Acts 14.17

THE BIRTH OF SAINT JOHN
THE BAPTIST
24 June

INTRODUCTORY SENTENCE

Blessed be the Lord God of Israel, for he has looked
favourably on his people and redeemed them.

Luke 1.68

or

There was a man sent from God, whose name was John;
he came as a witness to testify to the Light,
so that all might believe through him.

John 1.6–7

GOSPEL ACCLAMATION

Alleluia! **Alleluia!**
You, child, will be called the prophet of the Most High, for
you will go before the Lord to prepare his ways. **Alleluia!**

Luke 1.76

108

PRAYER AT THE PREPARATION OF THE TABLE

Blessed Lord God,
come to us your people in this holy sacrament
and set us free to worship you without fear
in holiness and righteousness all the days of our life;
through Jesus Christ our Lord.

JPY

COMMUNION SENTENCE

Among those born of women, no one is greater than John;
yet the least in the kingdom of God is greater than he.

Luke 7.28

SAINT PETER AND SAINT PAUL
THE APOSTLES
29 June

INTRODUCTORY SENTENCE

I will send them prophets and apostles, says the Lord,
some of whom they will kill and persecute.

Luke 11.49

or

You are built on the foundation of the apostles and prophets,
with Christ Jesus himself as the cornerstone.

Ephesians 2.20

or (where St Peter is celebrated alone)

The Lord indicated the kind of death by which Peter would
glorify God; after this he said to him, Follow me.

John 21.19

GOSPEL ACCLAMATION

Alleluia! **Alleluia!**
You are Simon, son of John; you are to be called Cephas.
Alleluia!

John 1.42

109

PRAYER AT THE PREPARATION OF THE TABLE

Lord Jesus, Shepherd of the sheep,
you know that we love you:
feed us your flock and help us always to follow you;
who are alive and reign, now and for ever.

JPY

or (where St Peter is celebrated alone)

God of grace, your Church is built on Peter's faith;
grant that like him we may be forgiven and restored,
overcome our weakness and serve you without wavering,
now and for ever.

NZPB*

COMMUNION SENTENCE

Keep watch over all the flock, of which the Holy Spirit has
made you overseers, to feed the Church of God which he
obtained with the blood of his own Son.

Acts 20.28*

or

Do you love me? says the Lord. Then feed my sheep.

John 21.17

SAINT THOMAS THE APOSTLE
3 July

INTRODUCTORY SENTENCE

Jesus said to Thomas,
If you know me, you will know my Father also;
from now on you do know him and have seen him.

John 14.7

GOSPEL ACCLAMATION

Alleluia! **Alleluia!**
These things are written that you may come to believe
that Jesus is the Christ, the Son of God. **Alleluia!**

John 20.31

PRAYER AT THE PREPARATION OF THE TABLE

Jesus, our Lord and our God,
after rising from the dead
    you broke bread with your apostles:
grant that in this holy sacrament
    we may know your resurrection;
who are alive and reign, now and for ever.

JPY

COMMUNION SENTENCE

Blessed are those who have not seen
and yet have come to believe.

John 20.29

SAINT MARY MAGDALENE
22 July

INTRODUCTORY SENTENCE

With Jesus were some women who had been cured of evil
spirits and infirmities: Mary called Magdalene and many
others, who provided for him out of their resources.

Luke 8.2–3

GOSPEL ACCLAMATION

Alleluia! **Alleluia!**
Jesus appeared first to Mary Magdalene;
she went out and told those who had been with him
that he was alive and had been seen by her. **Alleluia!**

Mark 16.9–11

PRAYER AT THE PREPARATION OF THE TABLE

Lord Jesus Christ,
grant that by the mystery of your body and blood,
we may watch at your cross, weep at your tomb
and witness to your resurrection;
who are alive and reign, now and for ever.

JPY

COMMUNION SENTENCE

Go quickly and tell his disciples:
Jesus has been raised from the dead.

Matthew 28.7

SAINT JAMES THE APOSTLE
25 July

INTRODUCTORY SENTENCE

Jesus saw James son of Zebedee and his brother John,
who were in the boat mending the nets;
immediately he called them;
and they left their father Zebedee in the boat
    with the hired men and followed him.

Mark 1.19–20

GOSPEL ACCLAMATION

Alleluia! **Alleluia!**
The greatest among you must become like the youngest,
says the Lord, and the leader like one who serves. **Alleluia!**

Luke 22.26

PRAYER AT THE PREPARATION OF THE TABLE

Grant, O Lord Jesus Christ,
that we may drink of your cup and share in your death,
and so be brought to the glory of your resurrection,
where you are alive and reign, now and for ever.

JPY

COMMUNION SENTENCE

You will sit on twelve thrones, judging the twelve tribes of
Israel; and everyone who has left houses or brothers or
sisters or father or mother or children or fields for my
name's sake will inherit eternal life.

Matthew 19.28–29

ANNE AND JOACHIM
26 July

INTRODUCTORY SENTENCE

Let your father and mother be glad;
let her who bore you rejoice.

Proverbs 23.25

or

Blessed are you, O Lord, God of our ancestors,
and to be praised and highly exalted for ever.

Azariah 29

GOSPEL ACCLAMATION

Alleluia! **Alleluia!**
The Lord has come to the help of his servant Israel,
mindful of his mercy, the promise he made to our ancestors.
Alleluia!

Luke 1.54–55

or

Alleluia! **Alleluia!**
My words shall not depart out of your mouth, says the Lord,
or out of the mouths of your children,
or out of the mouths of your children's children. **Alleluia!**

Isaiah 59.21

PRAYER AT THE PREPARATION OF THE TABLE

Dayspring of all mercy,
whose grace creates in our hearts
    the love you would have us offer:
grant us such faithfulness in the works that you command,
that we may be worthy to share in the banquet of your mercy;
through Jesus Christ our Lord.

FAS

COMMUNION SENTENCE

Honour your father and your mother,
as the Lord your God commanded you.

Deuteronomy 5.16

or

The merciful goodness of the Lord
endures for ever on those who fear him,
and his righteousness on children's children.

Psalm 103.17

MARY, MARTHA AND LAZARUS
29 July

INTRODUCTORY SENTENCE

If you believe, says the Lord, you will see the glory of God.

John 11.40

GOSPEL ACCLAMATION

Alleluia! **Alleluia!**
Jesus loved Martha and her sister and Lazarus. **Alleluia!**

John 11.5

PRAYER AT THE PREPARATION OF THE TABLE

Lord Jesus our resurrection:
grant us both to wait upon your coming to us
and to be ready to meet you,
both to serve you and to listen to you;
and let us be ready when you call us
    through death to your eternal life;
who are alive and reign, now and for ever.

JPY

COMMUNION SENTENCE

I am the resurrection and the life, says the Lord;
those who believe in me, even though they die, will live.

John 11.25

THE TRANSFIGURATION OF OUR LORD
6 August

INTRODUCTORY SENTENCE

Restore us, O Lord God of hosts; show the light of your
countenance and we shall be saved.

Psalm 80.19

GOSPEL ACCLAMATION

Alleluia! **Alleluia!**
This is my beloved Son, with him I am well pleased; listen to
him. **Alleluia!**

Matthew 17.5

PRAYER AT THE PREPARATION OF THE TABLE

Lord, as your Son was transfigured before the disciples,
may these gifts be made holy by the splendour of his glory
and our lives be transformed by his presence among us;
who is alive and reigns, now and for ever.

JPY

COMMUNION SENTENCE

God who said, 'Let light shine out of darkness,' has shone in
our hearts to give the light of the knowledge of the glory of
God in the face of Jesus Christ.

2 Corinthians 4.6

THE BLESSED VIRGIN MARY
15 August or (for pastoral reasons) 8 September

INTRODUCTORY SENTENCE

Greetings, favoured one, the Lord is with you; blessed are
you among women and blessed is the fruit of your womb.

Luke 1.28, 42

GOSPEL ACCLAMATION

Alleluia! **Alleluia!**
Blessed is she who believed that there would be a
fulfilment of what was spoken to her by the Lord. **Alleluia!**

Luke 1.45

PRAYER AT THE PREPARATION OF THE TABLE

God our Saviour,
whose mercy is from generation to generation:
in this sacrament may we share with our mother Mary
the fullness of joy in your kingdom;
through Jesus Christ our Lord.

JPY

COMMUNION SENTENCE

The Lord has lifted up the lowly;
he has filled the hungry with good things.

Luke 1.52–53

SAINT BARTHOLOMEW THE APOSTLE
24 August

INTRODUCTORY SENTENCE

Lord, you are the Son of God, you are the King of Israel!

John 1.49*

GOSPEL ACCLAMATION

Alleluia! **Alleluia!**
Whoever welcomes me welcomes the one who sent me,
says the Lord. **Alleluia!**

Luke 9.48

PRAYER AT THE PREPARATION OF THE TABLE

Jesus, Son of God and King of Israel,
grant us so to come to you,

to give ourselves in sincerity, faithfulness and truth,
that heaven itself may be opened to us
and that we may see you in your glory;
who are alive and reign, now and for ever.

JPY

COMMUNION SENTENCE

Blessed are those servants whom the Lord finds watching; he
will make them sit down at table and will come to serve them.

Luke 12.36

THE BEHEADING OF SAINT JOHN
THE BAPTIST
29 August

INTRODUCTORY SENTENCE

Herod the tetrarch added to all the evil things he had done
by shutting up John in prison.

Luke 3.19

or

The friend of the bridegroom
rejoices greatly at the bridegroom's voice;
therefore my joy has been fulfilled, said John;
he must increase, but I must decrease.

John 3.29–30

GOSPEL ACCLAMATION

Alleluia! **Alleluia!**
With many exhortations,
John proclaimed the good news to the people. **Alleluia!**

Luke 3.18

or

Alleluia! **Alleluia!**
You are my witnesses, said John, that I said, I am not the
Christ, but I have been sent ahead of him. **Alleluia!**

John 3.24, 28

117

PRAYER AT THE PREPARATION OF THE TABLE

O Lord our God,
by this holy sacrament save us from our adversary
and from the hand of all who hate us,
and guide us out of darkness and the shadow of death
into the way of peace, through Jesus Christ our Lord.

JPY

COMMUNION SENTENCE

John the Baptist has come eating no bread and drinking
no wine; the Son of Man has come eating and drinking;
Wisdom is justified by all her children.

Luke 7.33–35

or

John baptized with the baptism of repentance,
telling the people to believe in the one coming after him,
that is, in Jesus.

Acts 19.4

THE BIRTH OF THE BLESSED VIRGIN MARY
8 September

See also the Common of the Blessed Virgin Mary, page 133.

INTRODUCTORY SENTENCE

My heart exults in the Lord;
my strength is exalted in my God.

1 Samuel 2.1

or

The mercy of the Lord is for those who fear him
from generation to generation.

Luke 1.50

GOSPEL ACCLAMATION

Alleluia! **Alleluia!**
As a mother comforts her child, so I will comfort you; you
shall be comforted in Jerusalem. **Alleluia!**

Isaiah 66.13

or

Alleluia! **Alleluia!**
Here am I, the servant of the Lord; let it be with me
according to your word. **Alleluia!**

Luke 1.38

PRAYER AT THE PREPARATION OF THE TABLE

Heavenly Father,
the birth of your Son Jesus Christ
deepened his mother Mary's love for you
and increased her holiness:
may his sharing in our mortal nature
give us courage in our human weakness,
free us from our sins
and make the offering of our lives acceptable to you;
through the same Christ our Lord.

JPY from Roman Missal

COMMUNION SENTENCE

The Lord has lifted up the lowly; he has filled the hungry
with good things.

Luke 1.52–53

HOLY CROSS DAY
14 September

INTRODUCTORY SENTENCE

May I never boast of anything, except the cross of our Lord
Jesus Christ, by which the world has been crucified to me
and I to the world.

Galatians 6.14

119

GOSPEL ACCLAMATION

Alleluia! **Alleluia!**
The message about the cross is foolishness to those who are
perishing, but to us who are being saved it is the power of
God. **Alleluia!**

1 Corinthians 1.18

PRAYER AT THE PREPARATION OF THE TABLE

Lord Jesus Christ,
you were lifted high upon the cross,
to draw the whole world to yourself:
draw us to you in this holy sacrament,
that through the mystery of your body and blood
we may know again the triumph of your cross;
who are alive and reign, now and for ever.

JPY

COMMUNION SENTENCE

Through Christ God was pleased to reconcile to himself all
things, making peace through the blood of the cross.

Colossians 1.20

SAINT MATTHEW
THE APOSTLE AND EVANGELIST
21 September

INTRODUCTORY SENTENCE

The Son of Man came eating and drinking and they say,
'Look, a friend of tax-collectors and sinners!'
Yet Wisdom is vindicated by her deeds.

Matthew 11.19

GOSPEL ACCLAMATION

Alleluia! **Alleluia!**
The tax collectors are going into the kingdom of God ahead
of you, says the Lord, because they believed him. **Alleluia!**

Matthew 21.31–32*

PRAYER AT THE PREPARATION OF THE TABLE

Lord Jesus Christ,
who came not to call the righteous, but sinners:
grant us so to repent of our sins and to turn our hearts to you,
that we may be made welcome in the feast of your kingdom;
where you are alive and reign, now and for ever.

JPY

COMMUNION SENTENCE

Levi gave a great banquet for Jesus in his house;
and there was a large crowd of tax collectors and others
sitting at the table with them.

Luke 5.29

SAINT MICHAEL AND ALL ANGELS
29 September

INTRODUCTORY SENTENCE

Praise the Lord from the heavens; praise him in the heights!
Praise him all you angels of his; praise him all his host!

Psalm 148.1–2

GOSPEL ACCLAMATION

Alleluia! **Alleluia!**
I saw an angel flying in mid-heaven, with an eternal gospel
to proclaim to those who live on the earth, to every nation
and tribe and language and people. **Alleluia!**

Revelation 14.6

PRAYER AT THE PREPARATION OF THE TABLE

God of glory,
as you have appointed angels to minister in your presence,
so may all our worship bring you worthy praise;
through Jesus Christ our Lord.

BAS

121

COMMUNION SENTENCE

Mortals ate of the bread of angels;
the Lord gave food in abundance.

Psalm 78.25

SAINT LUKE THE EVANGELIST
18 October

INTRODUCTORY SENTENCE

How beautiful upon the mountains
are the feet of the messenger who announces peace,
who brings good news, who announces salvation.

Isaiah 52.7

GOSPEL ACCLAMATION

Alleluia! **Alleluia!**
Whoever listens to you listens to me, says the Lord. **Alleluia!**

Luke 10.16

PRAYER AT THE PREPARATION OF THE TABLE

God of compassion,
you are a strong tower for all who trust in you:
be now and evermore our defence,
that we may proclaim the only name under heaven
given for health and salvation,
even Jesus Christ our Lord.

BAS

COMMUNION SENTENCE

Go and proclaim the kingdom of God.

Luke 9.60

SAINT SIMON AND SAINT JUDE
THE APOSTLES
28 October

INTRODUCTORY SENTENCE

Beloved, contend for the faith that was once for all entrusted
to the saints.

Jude 3

or

The apostles went to the upper room where they were
staying: Peter and John and James and Andrew, Philip and
Thomas, Bartholomew and Matthew, James son of Alphaeus
and Simon the Zealot and Judas son of James; all these were
constantly devoting themselves prayer, together with certain
women, including Mary the mother of Jesus as well as his
brothers.

Acts 1.13–14

GOSPEL ACCLAMATION

Alleluia! **Alleluia!**
Remember the words of the apostles
  of our Lord Jesus Christ;
and build yourselves up on your most holy faith. **Alleluia!**

Jude 17, 20*

PRAYER AT THE PREPARATION OF THE TABLE

Lord Jesus Christ,
you shared this holy supper with your apostles:
keep us within the love of God
and by your mercy bring us to your eternal life;
who are alive and reign, now and for ever.

JPY

COMMUNION SENTENCE

Those who love me will keep my word, says the Lord;
my Father will love them
and we will come to them and make our home with them.

John 14.23

ALL SAINTS
1 November or Fourth Sunday before Advent

See pages 87–8.

COMMEMORATION OF THE FAITHFUL DEPARTED (ALL SOULS' DAY)
2 November

This provision may be used for the commemoration of the departed on other occasions.

During Eastertide 'Alleluia!' may be added to the introductory and communion sentences.

During Lent an alternative response should be used instead of 'alleluia!' in the gospel acclamation.

INTRODUCTORY SENTENCE

Rest eternal grant unto them, O Lord;
and let light perpetual shine upon them.

Traditional, cf. 2 Esdras 2.34–35*

or

We believe that Jesus died and rose again; even so, through
Jesus, God will bring with him those who have died.

1 Thessalonians 4.14

GOSPEL ACCLAMATION

Alleluia! **Alleluia!**
Anyone who hears my words and believes him who sent me
has eternal life, says the Lord, and does not come under
judgment, but has passed from death to life. **Alleluia!**

John 5.24

PRAYER AT THE PREPARATION OF THE TABLE

Almighty God,
grant that we, with all those who have believed in you,

may be united in the full knowledge of your love
and the unclouded vision of your glory;
through Jesus Christ our Lord.

ASB

COMMUNION SENTENCE

Anyone who eats my flesh and drinks my blood has eternal
life, says the Lord, and I shall raise him up on the last day.

John 6.54

DISMISSAL

[The Lord be with you;
And also with you.]
May they rest in peace;
And rise in glory.

IN EASTERTIDE:

May they rest in peace, alleluia!
And rise in glory, alleluia!

THE SAINTS AND MARTYRS
OF ENGLAND
8 November

INTRODUCTORY SENTENCE

Remember the deeds of the ancestors,
which they did in their generations;
and you will receive great honour and an everlasting name.

1 Maccabees 2.51

GOSPEL ACCLAMATION

Alleluia! **Alleluia!**
Blessed are you, O Lord, God of our ancestors, and worthy of
all praise; and glorious is your name for ever! **Alleluia!**

Azariah 3

PRAYER AT THE PREPARATION OF THE TABLE

God of our forebears:
turn our hearts from strife and jealousy
and make us love the works of peace,
that our lives may be ready
   to receive the abundance of your table;
through Jesus Christ our Lord.

FAS

COMMUNION SENTENCE

Faith is the assurance of things hoped for,
the conviction of things not seen;
indeed by faith our ancestors received approval.

Hebrews 11.1–2

SAINT ANDREW THE APOSTLE
30 November

INTRODUCTORY SENTENCE

Two of John's disciples came and saw where Jesus was
staying and they remained with him that day; one of the two
was Andrew, Simon Peter's brother.

John 1.39–40

GOSPEL ACCLAMATION

Alleluia! **Alleluia!**
Andrew found his brother and told him, 'We have found the
Messiah!' and he brought him to Jesus. **Alleluia!**

John 1.41–42

PRAYER AT THE PREPARATION OF THE TABLE

Lord Jesus Christ,
who took the bread which Andrew brought to you
and with it fed a great multitude:

grant that this bread, blessed and broken in your name
may satisfy our hunger for your eternal life,
who are alive and reign, now and for ever.

JPY

COMMUNION SENTENCE

Gather up the fragments left over,
so that nothing may be lost.

John 6.12

SAINT STEPHEN THE FIRST MARTYR
26 December

INTRODUCTORY SENTENCE

Thus says the Lord:
Heaven is my throne and the earth is my footstool,
all these things my hand has made;
but this is the one to whom I will look:
to the humble and contrite in spirit,
who trembles at my word.

Isaiah 66.1–2; cf. Acts 7.49

GOSPEL ACCLAMATION

Alleluia! **Alleluia!**
The word of God continued to spread; the number
of disciples increased greatly in Jerusalem. **Alleluia!**

Acts 6.7

PRAYER AT THE PREPARATION OF THE TABLE

Almighty God,
who called your servant Stephen
    to minister at table in your Church
and to bear witness for Christ even unto death:
grant that at this table we may be filled
    with your grace and power;
and so faithfully follow our Lord and Saviour Jesus Christ.

JPY

COMMUNION SENTENCE

This child is destined for the falling and for the rising
of many in Israel and to be a sign that will be opposed,
so that the inner thoughts of many will be revealed.

Luke 2.34–35

SAINT JOHN THE EVANGELIST
27 December

INTRODUCTORY SENTENCE

What was from the beginning, the Word who is life,
we declare to you.

1 John 1.1–2*

GOSPEL ACCLAMATION

Alleluia! **Alleluia!**
He who saw this has testified so that you also may believe;
his testimony is true and he knows that he tells the truth.
Alleluia!

John 21.24*

PRAYER AT THE PREPARATION OF THE TABLE

Jesus, new beginning, heavenly bread, living water:
we hear the word of life, we see and grasp the truth;
help us to proclaim it; for your name's sake.

NZPB*

COMMUNION SENTENCE

One of his disciples – the one whom Jesus loved –
was reclining next to him at supper.

John 13.23

THE HOLY INNOCENTS
28 December

INTRODUCTORY SENTENCE

Do not weep for me, says the Lord,
but weep for yourselves and for your children.

Luke 23.28

GOSPEL ACCLAMATION

Alleluia! **Alleluia!**
Whoever becomes humble like this little child
is the greatest in the kingdom of heaven. **Alleluia!**

Matthew 18.4

PRAYER AT THE PREPARATION OF THE TABLE

Heavenly Father,
you enfold us all in your love,
grant that in this eucharist
we may be fed with the bread of eternal life
which you have promised for all your children,
your Son Jesus Christ our Lord.

JPY

COMMUNION SENTENCE

Take care that you do not despise one of these little ones,
says the Lord; for in heaven their angels continually see the
face of my Father in heaven.

Matthew 18.10

DEDICATION FESTIVAL

See pages 85–6.

Common of Saints

_____ Common of Saints _____

Where alternatives are provided, sentences or prayers should be chosen with reference to other parts of the liturgy; in particular the acclamation should relate to the gospel reading.

In Lent the gospel acclamation should be amended by substituting alternative words for 'alleluia' as follows:
Praise be to the Lord Jesus!
[_scriptural text_]
Praise be to the Lord Jesus!

In Eastertide 'alleluia' may be added to any text where indicated in brackets.

THE BLESSED VIRGIN MARY

INTRODUCTORY SENTENCE

Greetings, favoured one! the Lord is with you [alleluia!], blessed are you among women and blessed is the fruit of your womb [alleluia, alleluia!].

Luke 1.28, 42

_or_

My heart exults in the Lord [alleluia!],
my strength is exalted in my God [alleluia, alleluia!].

1 Samuel 2.1

GOSPEL ACCLAMATION

See note on page 133.

Alleluia! **Alleluia!**
Here am I, the servant of the Lord;
let it be with me according to your word. **Alleluia!**

Luke 1.38

or

Alleluia! **Alleluia!**
Blessed is she who believed that there would be a fulfilment
of what was spoken to her by the Lord. **Alleluia!**

Luke 1.45

or

Alleluia! **Alleluia!**
As a mother comforts her child, so I will comfort you;
you shall be comforted in Jerusalem. **Alleluia!**

Isaiah 66.13

PRAYER AT THE PREPARATION OF THE TABLE

God our Saviour,
whose mercy is from generation to generation:
in this sacrament may we share with our mother Mary
the fullness of joy in your kingdom;
through Jesus Christ our Lord.

JPY

COMMUNION SENTENCE

The Lord has lifted up the lowly;
he has filled the hungry with good things [alleluia!].

Luke 1.52–53

APOSTLES AND EVANGELISTS

INTRODUCTORY SENTENCE

The disciples went out [alleluia!],
and proclaimed the good news everywhere [alleluia, alleluia!].

Mark 16.20

or

The apostles went to the upper room [alleluia!],
Peter and John and James and Andrew, Philip and Thomas,
Bartholomew and Matthew, James son of Alphaeus and
Simon the Zealot and Judas son of James [alleluia, alleluia!].

Acts 1.13–14

GOSPEL ACCLAMATION

See note on page 133.

Alleluia! **Alleluia!**
Remember the commandment of the Lord and Saviour
spoken through your apostles. **Alleluia!**

2 Peter 3.2

or

Alleluia! **Alleluia!**
The Lord has sent me to bring good news to the oppressed.
Alleluia!

Isaiah 61.1, cf Luke 4.18

PRAYER AT THE PREPARATION OF THE TABLE

Heavenly Father,
we have heard the good news of your Son Jesus Christ:
grant that as he shared this supper with his apostles,
he may keep us in the joy of his kingdom;
who is alive and reigns, now and for ever.

JPY

or

Lord Jesus Christ,
we have heard your apostles' teaching:
keep us united in their fellowship
by the breaking of this bread,
we make our prayer in your name.

JPY

135

COMMUNION SENTENCE

Blessed are those servants whom the master finds alert when he comes; he will have them sit down to eat and he will come and serve them [alleluia!].

Luke 12.37*

or

You shall eat and drink at my table in my kingdom, says the Lord, and sit on thrones judging the twelve tribes of Israel [alleluia!].

Luke 22.30*

MARTYRS

INTRODUCTORY SENTENCE

You will be hated by all because of my name, says the Lord
  [alleluia!],
but the one who endures to the end will be saved
  [alleluia, alleluia!].

Matthew 10.22

GOSPEL ACCLAMATION

See note on page 133.

Alleluia! **Alleluia!**
Those who lose their life for the sake of the gospel
will save it. **Alleluia!**

Mark 8.35

PRAYER AT THE PREPARATION OF THE TABLE

Father,
inspire us with the memory of your martyr *N*,
nourish us with the bread of life
and give us courage to witness with our lives
to the victory of your Son Jesus Christ;
who is alive and reigns, now and for ever.

BAS*

or

Jesus our Redeemer,
you gave your life to ransom us;
grant us faith and resolution,
that we may drink your cup and undergo your baptism;
who are alive and reign, now and for ever.

NZPB*

COMMUNION SENTENCE

You have stood by me in my trials;
you will eat and drink at my table in my kingdom [alleluia!].

Luke 22.28, 30

or

The cup that I drink you will drink; but to sit at my right
hand or at my left is for those for whom it has been prepared
[alleluia!].

Mark 10.39–40

TEACHERS OF THE FAITH

INTRODUCTORY SENTENCE

Let the elders who rule well be considered worthy of double
honour [alleluia!], especially those who labour in preaching
and teaching [alleluia, alleluia!].

1 Timothy 5.17

or

Hold to the standard of sound teaching that you have heard
from me [alleluia!], in the faith and love that are in Christ
Jesus [alleluia, alleluia!].

2 Timothy 1.13

GOSPEL ACCLAMATION

See note on page 133.

Alleluia! **Alleluia!**
Go and make disciples of all nations, says the Lord, teaching
them to obey everything that I have commanded you.
Alleluia!

Matthew 28.19–20

or

137

Alleluia! **Alleluia!**
Whoever does these commandments and teaches them
will be called great in the kingdom of heaven. **Alleluia!**

Matthew 5.19

PRAYER AT THE PREPARATION OF THE TABLE

Lord, your Spirit leads us into all truth:
build us up in the faith once delivered to the saints;
and keep our eyes fixed on you;
who are alive and reign, now and for ever.

JPY

or

O God,
your Word is the light of our pilgrimage,
the end and fulfilment of our knowledge:
grant that as we await in love the dawning of his radiance,
we may know him in the breaking of this bread;
we ask this through him who is alive and reigns,
now and for ever.

BAS*

COMMUNION SENTENCE

Whoever holds to the law will obtain wisdom;
she will feed him with the bread of learning
and give him the water of wisdom to drink [alleluia!].

Sirach 15.1, 3

or

Those who are taught the word must share in all good things
with their teacher [alleluia!].

Galatians 6.6

BISHOPS AND OTHER PASTORS

INTRODUCTORY SENTENCE

Keep watch over yourselves and over all the flock, of which
the Holy Spirit has made you overseers [alleluia!], to
shepherd the church of God that he obtained with the blood
of his own Son [alleluia, alleluia!].

Acts 20.28

or

A bishop must be above reproach [alleluia!], married only
once, temperate, sensible, respectable, hospitable, and an apt
teacher [alleluia, alleluia!].

1 Timothy 3.2

or

Let your priests be clothed with righteousness [alleluia!],
let your faithful people sing with joy [alleluia, alleluia!].

Psalm 132.9

GOSPEL ACCLAMATION

See note on page 133.

Alleluia! **Alleluia!**
I will give you shepherds after my own heart, who will feed
you with knowledge and understanding. **Alleluia!**

Jeremiah 3.15

PRAYER AT THE PREPARATION OF THE TABLE

Shepherd of Israel, your flock is never without care:
grant that your Church may always rejoice in faithful pastors,
who are servants of Christ and stewards of your mysteries;
we ask this through Jesus Christ our Lord.

BAS*

or

Good Shepherd, King of love:
may our care for each other grow constantly
   more reverent and discerning;
we ask this through Jesus Christ our Lord.

NZPB*

COMMUNION SENTENCE

He will feed his flock like a shepherd;
he will gather the lambs in his arms
  and carry them in his bosom
and gently lead the mother sheep [alleluia!].

Isaiah 40.11

RELIGIOUS

INTRODUCTORY SENTENCE

Prepare your minds for action;
discipline yourselves [alleluia!],
set all your hope on the grace that Jesus Christ will bring you
when he is revealed [alleluia, alleluia!].

1 Peter 1.13

or

Be serious and discipline yourselves
for the sake of your prayers [alleluia!].

1 Peter 4.7

GOSPEL ACCLAMATION

See note on page 133.

Alleluia! **Alleluia!**
My heart stands in awe of your word; seven times a day do I
praise you, because of your righteous judgments. **Alleluia!**

Psalm 119.161, 164

PRAYER AT THE PREPARATION OF THE TABLE

Jesus, Son of God,
grant us a readiness to strive for holiness
and an obedience to suffer for the joy of being one with you;
who are alive and reign, now and for ever.

NZPB*

or

God our Father,
grant that we may be on fire
    with your spirit of discipline and love;
through Jesus Christ our Lord.

APB*

COMMUNION SENTENCE

Taste and see that the Lord is good;
happy are they who trust in him [alleluia!].

Psalm 34.8

MISSIONARIES

INTRODUCTORY SENTENCE

Declare his glory among the nations [alleluia!],
and his wonders among all peoples [alleluia, alleluia!].

Psalm 96.3

GOSPEL ACCLAMATION

See note on page 133.

Alleluia! **Alleluia!**
This good news of the kingdom will be proclaimed
throughout the world, as a testimony to all the nations.
Alleluia!

Matthew 24.14

or

Alleluia! **Alleluia!**
Repentance and forgiveness of sins is to be proclaimed
in Christ's name to all nations. **Alleluia!**

Luke 24.47

PRAYER AT THE PREPARATION OF THE TABLE

God of our salvation,
your love for all the world is endless:

may our worship today renew our dedication
    to your mission;
in the name of Jesus Christ our Lord.

*BAS**

or

God our Father,
who called us out of darkness into your marvellous light:
shine in our hearts and enable us to proclaim your love;
through Jesus Christ our Lord.

*APB**

COMMUNION SENTENCE

You will be my witnesses to the ends of the earth,
says the Lord [alleluia!].

Acts 1.8

ANY SAINT

INTRODUCTORY SENTENCE

Love the Lord, all you his saints [alleluia!],
the Lord protects the faithful [alleluia, alleluia!].

Psalm 31.23

or

The mouth of the righteous utters wisdom [alleluia!],
and their tongue speaks what is right [alleluia, alleluia!].

Psalm 37.30

or

The holy ones of the Most High shall receive the kingdom
    [alleluia!],
and possess the kingdom for ever and ever [alleluia, alleluia!].

Daniel 7.18

or

Be imitators of God, as beloved children [alleluia!],
and live in love as Christ loved us [alleluia, alleluia!].

Ephesians 5.1–2

GOSPEL ACCLAMATION

See note on page 133.

Alleluia! **Alleluia!**
Blessed are those who hear the word of God and obey it.
Alleluia!

Luke 11.28

or

Alleluia! **Alleluia!**
We bring you the good news that what God promised to our
ancestors he has fulfilled for us their children. **Alleluia!**

Acts 32–33

or

Alleluia! **Alleluia!**
You have love for all the saints because of the hope laid up
for you in heaven; of which you have heard in the gospel.
Alleluia!

Colossians 1.4–5*

or

Alleluia! **Alleluia!**
God called you through our proclamation of the good news,
so that you may obtain the glory of our Lord Jesus Christ.
Alleluia!

2 Thessalonians 2.14

PRAYER AT THE PREPARATION OF THE TABLE

Lord Jesus Christ, King of glory,
you have opened the kingdom of heaven to all believers:
come and help your people by the mystery
    of your body and blood;
and bring us with your saints to your eternal glory;
who are alive and reign, now and for ever.

JPY based on Te Deum laudamus

or

God of love and justice,
you make known your ways in the lives of your saints:
as we seek to follow their example,
help us to know your holy will and to do it;
through Jesus Christ our Lord.

BAS*

143

or

God of glory,
let this table be a foretaste of the kingdom of your Son:
may we be faithful to him in this life
and rejoice with your servant *N* for ever;
through Jesus Christ our Lord.

BAS*

COMMUNION SENTENCE

People will come from east and west, from north and south
and will eat in the kingdom of God [alleluia!].

Luke 13.29

or

When you give a banquet, invite the poor, the crippled,
the lame and the blind and you will be blessed,
because they cannot repay you, for you will be repaid
at the resurrection of the righteous [alleluia!].

Luke 14.13–14

or

These are they who have come out of the great ordeal;
they have washed their robes and made them white
in the blood of the Lamb [alleluia!].

Revelation 7.14

Special Occasions

_____ Special Occasions _____

See notes on page 133.

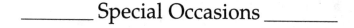

MOTHERING SUNDAY

See pages 31–2.

THE GUIDANCE OF THE HOLY SPIRIT

See also the provision for Pentecost, pages 49–50.

INTRODUCTORY SENTENCE

When the Spirit of truth comes,
he will guide you into all the truth [alleluia!].

John 16.13

GOSPEL ACCLAMATION
See note on page 133.

Alleluia! **Alleluia!**
The Holy Spirit fell on all who heard the word. **Alleluia!**

Acts 10.44

or

Alleluia! **Alleluia!**
Our message of the gospel came to you not in word only,
but also in power and in the Holy Spirit
and with full conviction. **Alleluia!**

1 Thessalonians 1.5

PRAYER AT THE PREPARATION OF THE TABLE

Spirit of God, you are the breath of creation,
the wind of change that blows through our lives,
opening us up to new dreams and new hopes,
    new life in Jesus Christ:
by your power at work in us may we be open to your love
and open for the service of the world;
through Jesus Christ our Lord.

PPCW*

COMMUNION SENTENCE

The grace of the Lord Jesus Christ, the love of God and the
communion of the Holy Spirit be with all of you [alleluia!].

2 Corinthians 13.13

or

Guard the good treasure entrusted to you,
with the help of the Holy Spirit living in us [alleluia!].

2 Timothy 1.14

ROGATION DAYS

INTRODUCTORY SENTENCE

As long as the earth endures, seedtime and harvest,
cold and heat, summer and winter, day and night,
shall not cease [alleluia!].

Genesis 8.22

GOSPEL ACCLAMATION

See note on page 133.

Alleluia! **Alleluia!**
These are the ones sown on the good soil:
they hear the word of God and accept it and bear fruit,
thirty and sixty and a hundredfold. **Alleluia!**

Mark 4.20

PRAYER AT THE PREPARATION OF THE TABLE

Living God, maker of heaven and earth,
you have fed us with the good news of your love;
as we come to seek the living Word, your Son Jesus Christ,
feed us the bread of life and fill our hearts with joy;
through him who is alive and reigns, now and for ever.

JPY based on Acts 14.15–17

COMMUNION SENTENCE

The eyes of all look to you, O Lord;
and you give them their food in due season [alleluia!].

Psalm 145.15

HARVEST THANKSGIVING

INTRODUCTORY SENTENCE

Look around you
and see how the fields are ripe for harvesting.

John 4.35

or

The earth has yielded its increase;
God our God has blessed us.

Psalm 67.6

GOSPEL ACCLAMATION

Alleluia! **Alleluia!**
We bring you good news, that you should turn to the living
God, who gives you rains from heaven and fruitful seasons,
filling you with food and your hearts with joy. **Alleluia!**

Acts 14.15, 17*

149

PRAYER AT THE PREPARATION OF THE TABLE

Creator God, maker of all things,
patient Father, awakener of our love:
accept these gifts and our joy in offering them;
through Jesus Christ our Lord.

PPCW

or

Source of all life, the heaven and earth are yours,
yet you have given us dominion over all things:
receive the symbols of our labour and love
which we offer you this day,
in the name of Jesus Christ our Lord.

BAS

COMMUNION SENTENCE

Lord, you bring forth food from the earth
and wine to gladden the human heart,
oil to make the face shine
    and bread to strengthen the human heart.

Psalm 104.14–15

or

Eat your bread with enjoyment and drink your wine with a
    merry heart.

Ecclesiastes 9.7

THE PEACE OF THE WORLD

INTRODUCTORY SENTENCE

Pray for the peace of Jerusalem [alleluia!]:
Peace be within your walls and security within your towers
    [alleluia, alleluia!].

Psalm 122.6–7

GOSPEL ACCLAMATION

See note on page 133.

Alleluia! **Alleluia!**
How beautiful upon the mountains
are the feet of the messenger who announces peace,
who brings good news. **Alleluia!**

Isaiah 52.7

or

Alleluia! **Alleluia!**
Put on whatever will make you ready
to proclaim the gospel of peace. **Alleluia!**

Ephesians 6.15

PRAYER AT THE PREPARATION OF THE TABLE

O God, the author of peace and lover of concord,
to know you is eternal life, to serve you is perfect freedom:
defend us your servants from all assaults of our enemies,
that we may trust in your defence
    and not fear the power of any adversaries;
through Jesus Christ our Lord.

ASB

COMMUNION SENTENCE

The Lord grants peace within your borders;
he fills you with the finest of wheat [alleluia!].

Psalm 147.14

SOCIAL JUSTICE AND RESPONSIBILITY

INTRODUCTORY SENTENCE

The Lord loves righteousness and justice [alleluia!],
the earth is full of the steadfast love of the Lord
    [alleluia, alleluia!].

Psalm 33.5

GOSPEL ACCLAMATION

See note on page 133.

Alleluia! **Alleluia!**
The Lord has sent me to bring good news to the oppressed,
to bind up the broken hearted,
to proclaim liberty to captives and release to the prisoners,
to proclaim the year of the Lord's favour. **Alleluia!**

Isaiah 61.1–2

PRAYER AT THE PREPARATION OF THE TABLE

Accept, O Lord, the offering we seek to make;
and grant that we may ever work and pray
to build a world of peace and justice, of joy and freedom;
through Jesus Christ our Lord.

BCO*

COMMUNION SENTENCE

The Lord has lifted up the lowly;
he has filled the hungry with good things [alleluia!].

Luke 1.52–53

or

He who supplies seed to the sower and bread for food
will increase the harvest of your righteousness [alleluia!].

2 Corinthians 9.10

THE UNITY OF THE CHURCH

INTRODUCTORY SENTENCE

May God grant you to live in harmony with one another, in accordance with Christ Jesus [alleluia!], so that together you may with one voice glorify the God and Father of our Lord Jesus Christ [alleluia, alleluia!].

Romans 15.5–6

If there is any encouragement in Christ,
any consolation from love, any sharing in the Spirit [alleluia!],
be of the same mind, having the same love,
being in full accord and of one mind [alleluia, alleluia!].

Philippians 2.1–2

GOSPEL ACCLAMATION
See note on page 133.

Alleluia! **Alleluia!**
There will be one flock, one shepherd. **Alleluia!**

John 10.16

or

Alleluia! **Alleluia!**
Sanctify them in the truth; your word is truth. **Alleluia!**

John 17.17

PRAYER AT THE PREPARATION OF THE TABLE

God of power and love,
by your Holy Spirit,
draw the scattered flock of Christ into a visible unity
and make your Church a sign of hope to our divided world;
through Jesus Christ our Lord.

BCO

COMMUNION SENTENCE

Because there is one bread, we who are many are one body,
for we all partake of the one bread [alleluia!].

1 Corinthians 10.17

MISSION AND EVANGELISM

INTRODUCTORY SENTENCE

The Lord has sent me to bring good news to the oppressed,
to bind up the broken-hearted [alleluia!],
to proclaim liberty to captives and release to the prisoners;
to proclaim the year of the Lord's favour [alleluia, alleluia!].

Isaiah 61.1–2

GOSPEL ACCLAMATION

See note on page 133.

Alleluia! **Alleluia!**
Go into all the world and proclaim the good news
to the whole creation. **Alleluia!**

Mark 16.15

PRAYER AT THE PREPARATION OF THE TABLE

Loving God,
you sent your Son into the world
    that all might live through him:
pour out your Holy Spirit on your Church,
that she may proclaim to all people
    the gospel of the love of Christ,
till all are gathered into your kingdom
and your glory covers the earth as the waters fill the sea;
we ask this in the name of Jesus Christ our Lord.

BCO*

COMMUNION SENTENCE

The promise is for you, for your children
and for all who are far away,
everyone whom the Lord our God calls to him [alleluia!].

Acts 2.39

MINISTRY
including Ember Days

INTRODUCTORY SENTENCE

Let your priests be clothed with righteousness [alleluia!],
and let your faithful shout for joy [alleluia, alleluia!].

Psalm 132.9

or

The blind receive their sight, the lame walk,
the lepers are cleansed [alleluia!],
the deaf hear, the dead are raised
and the poor have good news brought to them
[alleluia, alleluia!].

Matthew 11.5

or

The harvest is plentiful but the labourers are few [alleluia!],
therefore ask the Lord of the harvest
to send out labourers into his harvest [alleluia!].

Luke 10.2

GOSPEL ACCLAMATION

See note on page 133.

Alleluia! **Alleluia!**
They departed and went through the villages, bringing the
good news and curing diseases everywhere. **Alleluia!**

Luke 9.6

or

Alleluia! **Alleluia!**
Father, sanctify them in the truth; your word is truth.
Alleluia!

John 17.17

or

Alleluia! **Alleluia!**
Of this gospel I have become a servant
according to the gift of God's grace that was given me
by the working of his power. **Alleluia!**

Ephesians 3.7

155

PRAYER AT THE PREPARATION OF THE TABLE

Remember, O Lord,
what you have wrought in us and not what we deserve;
and as you have called us to your service,
make us worthy of our calling;
through Jesus Christ our Lord.

1928 PB*

COMMUNION SENTENCE

Peace be with you, says the Lord;
as the Father has sent me, so I send you [alleluia!].

John 20.21

or

Do you love me? says the Lord; then feed my sheep [alleluia!].

John 21.17

or

Think of us in this way, as servants of Christ
and stewards of God's mysteries [alleluia!].

1 Corinthians 4.1

IN TIME OF TROUBLE

INTRODUCTORY SENTENCE

In my distress I called upon the Lord,
to my God I called [alleluia!],
from his temple he heard my voice
and my cry came to his ears [alleluia, alleluia!].

2 Samuel 22.7

or

The Lord is good, a stronghold on a day of trouble [alleluia],
he protects those who take refuge in him [alleluia, alleluia!].

Nahum 1.7

GOSPEL ACCLAMATION

See note on page 133.

Alleluia! **Alleluia!**
I wait for the Lord, my soul waits; and in his word I hope.
Alleluia!

Psalm 130.5

or

Alleluia! **Alleluia!**
In spite of persecution you received the word with joy
inspired by the Holy Spirit. **Alleluia!**

1 Thessalonians 1.6

PRAYER AT THE PREPARATION OF THE TABLE

Eternal God,
comfort of the afflicted and healer of the broken:
feed us at this table of life and hope,
and teach us the ways of gentleness and peace,
through your Son Jesus Christ our Lord.

BAS*

COMMUNION SENTENCE

You will weep and mourn, but the world will rejoice;
you will have pain, but your pain will turn into joy [alleluia!].

John 16.20

FOR THE SOVEREIGN

INTRODUCTORY SENTENCE

Give the king your justice, O God [alleluia!],
may he judge your people with righteousness
    [alleluia, alleluia!].

Psalm 72.1–2

or

Kings of the earth and all peoples,
princes and all rulers of the earth [alleluia!],
let them praise the name of the Lord [alleluia, alleluia!].

Psalm 148.11, 13

157

GOSPEL ACCLAMATION

See note on page 133.

Alleluia! **Alleluia!**
Now, you kings, be wise; be warned, O rulers of the earth.
Alleluia!

Psalm 2.10

or

Alleluia! **Alleluia!**
Hear the word of the Lord, O King,
you and your servants and your people. **Alleluia!**

Jeremiah 22.2

PRAYER AT THE PREPARATION OF THE TABLE

Lord Jesus Christ,
enthroned at the right hand of the Majesty on high,
rule in the hearts of all
and bring the whole world to worship at your feet;
who are alive and reign, now and for ever.

JPY

COMMUNION SENTENCE

The kingdom of heaven may be compared to a king
who gave a wedding banquet [alleluia!].

Matthew 22.2

or

Blessed is anyone who will eat bread in the kingdom of God
[alleluia!].

Luke 14.15

Part 2

Collects and Post-Communion Prayers

AUTHORIZED TEXTS

The Seasons

Advent

THE FIRST SUNDAY OF ADVENT

COLLECT

Almighty God,
give us grace to cast away the works of darkness
and to put on the armour of light,
now in the time of this mortal life,
in which your Son Jesus Christ
     came to us in great humility;
so that on the last day,
when he shall come again in his glorious majesty
     to judge the living and the dead,
we may rise to the life immortal;
through him who is alive and reigns with you
in the unity of the Holy Spirit,
one God, now and for ever.

*This prayer may be said as the post-communion prayer on any
day in Advent when it is not used as the collect.*

POST-COMMUNION PRAYER

O Lord our God,
make us watchful and keep us faithful
as we await the coming of your Son our Lord;
that, when he shall appear,
he may not find us sleeping in sin
but active in his service
and joyful in his praise;
through Jesus Christ our Lord.

THE SECOND SUNDAY OF ADVENT

COLLECT

O Lord, raise up, we pray, your power
and come among us,
and with great might succour us;
that whereas, through our sins and wickedness
we are grievously hindered
in running the race that is set before us,
your bountiful grace and mercy
may speedily help and deliver us;
through Jesus Christ your Son our Lord,
to whom with you and the Holy Spirit,
be honour and glory, now and for ever.

POST-COMMUNION PRAYER

Father in heaven,
who sent your Son to redeem the world
and will send him again to be our judge:
give us grace so to imitate him
    in the humility and purity of his first coming
that, when he comes again,
we may be ready to greet him
with joyful love and firm faith;
through Jesus Christ our Lord.

THE THIRD SUNDAY OF ADVENT

COLLECT

O Lord Jesus Christ,
who at your first coming sent your messenger
to prepare your way before you:
grant that the ministers and stewards of your mysteries
may likewise so prepare and make ready your way
by turning the hearts of the disobedient
    to the wisdom of the just,
that at your second coming to judge the world
we may be found an acceptable people in your sight;
for you are alive and reign with the Father
in the unity of the Holy Spirit,
one God, now and for ever.

POST-COMMUNION PRAYER

We give you thanks, O Lord, for these heavenly gifts;
kindle in us the fire of your Spirit
that when your Christ comes again
we may shine as lights before his face;
who is alive and reigns now and for ever.

THE FOURTH SUNDAY OF ADVENT

COLLECT

God our redeemer,
who prepared the Blessed Virgin Mary
to be the mother of your Son:
grant that, as she looked for his coming as our saviour,
so we may be ready to greet him
when he comes to be our judge;
who is alive and reigns with you
in the unity of the Holy Spirit,
one God, now and for ever.

POST-COMMUNION PRAYER

Heavenly Father,
who chose the Blessed Virgin Mary
to be the mother of the promised saviour:
fill us your servants with your grace,
that in all things we may embrace your holy will
and with her rejoice in your salvation;
through Jesus Christ our Lord.

Christmas

CHRISTMAS DAY

COLLECT

AT NIGHT

Eternal God,
who made this most holy night
to shine with the brightness of your one true light:
bring us, who have known the revelation
    of that light on earth,
to see the radiance of your heavenly glory;
through Jesus Christ your Son our Lord,
who is alive and reigns with you
in the unity of the Holy Spirit,
one God, now and for ever.

IN THE DAY

Almighty God,
you have given us your only-begotten Son
to take our nature upon him
and as at this time to be born of a pure virgin:
grant that we, who have been born again
and made your children by adoption and grace,
may daily be renewed by your Holy Spirit;
through Jesus Christ your Son our Lord,
who is alive and reigns with you
in the unity of the Holy Spirit,
one God, now and for ever.

POST-COMMUNION PRAYER

AT NIGHT

God our Father,
in this night you have made known to us again
the coming of our Lord Jesus Christ:
confirm our faith and fix our eyes on him
until the day dawns
and Christ the Morning Star rises in our hearts.
To him be glory both now and for ever.

IN THE DAY

God our Father,
whose Word has come among us
in the Holy Child of Bethlehem:
may the light of faith illumine our hearts
    and shine in our words and deeds;
through him who is Christ the Lord.

THE FIRST SUNDAY OF CHRISTMAS

COLLECT

Almighty God,
who wonderfully created us in your own image
and yet more wonderfully restored us
through your Son Jesus Christ:
grant that, as he came to share in our humanity,
so we may share the life of his divinity;
who is alive and reigns with you
in the unity of the Holy Spirit,
one God, now and for ever.

POST-COMMUNION PRAYER

Heavenly Father,
whose blessed Son shared at Nazareth
    the life of an earthly home:
help your Church to live as one family,
united in love and obedience,
and bring us at last to our home in heaven;
through Jesus Christ our Lord.

THE SECOND SUNDAY OF CHRISTMAS

COLLECT

Almighty God,
in the birth of your Son
you have poured on us the new light of your incarnate Word,
and shown us the fullness of your love:
help us to walk in his light and dwell in his love
that we may know the fullness of his joy;
who is alive and reigns with you
in the unity of the Holy Spirit,
one God, now and for ever.

POST-COMMUNION PRAYER

All praise to you,
almighty God and heavenly King,
who sent your Son into the world
to take our nature upon him
and to be born of a pure virgin:
grant that, as we are born again in him,
so he may continually dwell in us
and reign on earth as he reigns in heaven,
now and for ever.

_____ Epiphany_____

THE EPIPHANY

6 January

COLLECT

O God,
who by the leading of a star
manifested your only Son to the peoples of the earth:
mercifully grant that we,
who know you now by faith,
may at last behold your glory face to face;
through Jesus Christ your Son our Lord,
who is alive and reigns with you
in the unity of the Holy Spirit,
one God, now and for ever.

POST-COMMUNION PRAYER

Lord God,
the bright splendour whom the nations seek:
may we who with the wise men have been drawn
    by your light
discern the glory of your presence in your Son,
the Word made flesh, Jesus Christ our Lord.

THE BAPTISM OF CHRIST

First Sunday of Epiphany
or Monday 7 January, when 6 January is a Sunday

COLLECT

Almighty God,
who at the baptism of Jesus
revealed him to be your Son,
anointing him with the Holy Spirit:
grant to us, who are born again by water and the Spirit,
that we may be faithful to our calling
   as your adopted children;
through Jesus Christ your Son our Lord,
who is alive and reigns with you
in the unity of the Holy Spirit,
one God, now and for ever.

POST-COMMUNION PRAYER

Lord of all time and eternity,
you opened the heavens and revealed yourself as Father
in the baptism of Jesus your beloved Son:
by the power of your Spirit
complete the heavenly work of our rebirth
through the waters of the new creation;
through Jesus Christ our Lord.

THE SECOND SUNDAY OF EPIPHANY

COLLECT
Almighty God,
in Christ you make all things new:
transform the poverty of our nature by the riches of your
   grace,
and in the renewal of our lives

make known your heavenly glory;
through Jesus Christ your Son our Lord,
who is alive and reigns with you
in the unity of the Holy Spirit,
one God, now and for ever.

POST-COMMUNION PRAYER

God of glory,
you nourish us with your Word
who is the bread of life:
fill us with your Holy Spirit
that through us the light of your glory
may shine in all the world.
We ask this in the name of Jesus Christ our Lord.

THE THIRD SUNDAY OF EPIPHANY

COLLECT

Almighty God,
whose Son revealed in signs and miracles
the wonder of your saving presence:
renew your people with your heavenly grace,
and in all our weakness
sustain us by your mighty power;
through Jesus Christ your Son our Lord,
who is alive and reigns with you
in the unity of the Holy Spirit,
one God, now and for ever.

POST-COMMUNION PRAYER

Almighty Father,
whose Son our Saviour Jesus Christ is the light of the world:

may your people,
illumined by your word and sacraments,
shine with the radiance of his glory,
that he may be known, worshipped, and obeyed
    to the ends of the earth;
for he is alive and reigns, now and for ever.

THE FOURTH SUNDAY OF EPIPHANY

COLLECT

God our creator,
who in the beginning
commanded the light to shine out of darkness:
we pray that the light of the glorious gospel of Christ
may dispel the darkness of ignorance and unbelief,
shine into the hearts of all your people,
and reveal the knowledge of your glory
    in the face of Jesus Christ your Son our Lord,
who is alive and reigns with you
in the unity of the Holy Spirit,
one God, now and for ever.

POST-COMMUNION PRAYER

Generous Lord,
in word and eucharist we have proclaimed
    the mystery of your love:
help us so to live out our days,
that we may be signs of your wonders in the world;
through Jesus Christ our Saviour.

THE PRESENTATION OF CHRIST IN THE TEMPLE (CANDLEMAS)

2 February or the Sunday nearest 31 January

COLLECT

Almighty and ever-living God,
clothed in majesty,
whose beloved Son
    was this day presented in the Temple,
in substance of our flesh:
grant that we may be presented to you
    with pure and clean hearts,
by your Son Jesus Christ our Lord,
who is alive and reigns with you
in the unity of the Holy Spirit,
one God, now and for ever.

POST-COMMUNION PRAYER

Lord, you fulfilled the hope of Simeon and Anna,
who lived to welcome the Messiah:
may we, who have received these gifts beyond words,
prepare to meet Christ Jesus when he comes
    to bring us to eternal life;
for he is alive and reigns, now and for ever.

Ordinary Time

The provision for the last two Sundays before Lent is always used (see pages 175–6).

The prayers of the third, fourth and fifth Sundays before Lent and the lectionary of Propers 1 to 3 are used only as necessary, when there are more than two Sundays between Candlemas and Ash Wednesday.

THE FIFTH SUNDAY BEFORE LENT

COLLECT

Almighty God,
by whose grace alone we are accepted
    and called to your service:
strengthen us by your Holy Spirit
and make us worthy of our calling;
through Jesus Christ your Son our Lord,
who is alive and reigns with you
in the unity of the Holy Spirit,
one God, now and for ever.

POST-COMMUNION PRAYER

God of truth,
we have seen with our eyes
    and touched with our hands the bread of life:
strengthen our faith
that we may grow in love for you and for each other;
through Jesus Christ our Lord.

THE FOURTH SUNDAY BEFORE LENT

COLLECT

O God,
you know us to be set
in the midst of so many and great dangers,
that by reason of the frailty of our nature
we cannot always stand upright:
grant to us such strength and protection
as may support us in all dangers
and carry us through all temptations;
through Jesus Christ your Son our Lord,
who is alive and reigns with you
in the unity of the Holy Spirit,
one God, now and for ever.

POST-COMMUNION PRAYER

Go before us, O Lord, in all we do
with your most gracious favour,
and guide us with your continual help,
that in all our works
begun, continued and ended in you,
we may glorify your holy name,
and finally by your mercy receive everlasting life;
through Jesus Christ our Lord.

THE THIRD SUNDAY BEFORE LENT

COLLECT

Almighty God,
who alone can bring order
to the unruly wills and passions of sinful humanity:
give your people grace
so to love what you command
and to desire what you promise,
that, among the many changes of the world,

our hearts may surely there be fixed
where true joys are to be found;
through Jesus Christ your Son our Lord,
who is alive and reigns with you
in the unity of the Holy Spirit,
one God, now and for ever.

POST-COMMUNION PRAYER

Merciful Father,
who gave Jesus Christ to be for us the bread of life,
that those who come to him should never hunger:
draw us to the Lord in faith and love,
that we may eat and drink with him
at his table in the kingdom,
where he is alive and reigns, now and for ever.

THE SECOND SUNDAY BEFORE LENT

COLLECT

Almighty God,
you have created the heavens and the earth
and made us in your own image:
teach us to discern your hand in all your works
and your likeness in all your children;
through Jesus Christ your Son our Lord,
who with you and the Holy Spirit
    reigns supreme over all things,
now and for ever.

POST-COMMUNION PRAYER

God our creator,
by your gift
the tree of life was set at the heart of the earthly paradise,

and the bread of life at the heart of your Church:
may we who have been nourished at your table on earth
be transformed by the glory of the Saviour's cross
and enjoy the delights of eternity;
through Jesus Christ our Lord.

THE SUNDAY NEXT BEFORE LENT

COLLECT

Almighty Father,
whose Son was revealed in majesty
before he suffered death upon the cross:
give us grace to perceive his glory,
that we may be strengthened to suffer with him
and be changed into his likeness from glory to glory;
who is alive and reigns with you
in the unity of the Holy Spirit,
one God, now and for ever.

POST-COMMUNION PRAYER

Holy God,
we see your glory in the face of Jesus Christ:
may we who are partakers at his table
reflect his life in word and deed,
that all the world may know
    his power to change and save.
This we ask through Jesus Christ our Lord.

_____ Lent _____

ASH WEDNESDAY

COLLECT

Almighty and everlasting God,
you hate nothing that you have made
and forgive the sins of all those who are penitent:
 create and make in us new and contrite hearts
that we, worthily lamenting our sins
and acknowledging our wretchedness,
may receive from you, the God of all mercy,
perfect remission and forgiveness;
through Jesus Christ your Son our Lord,
who is alive and reigns with you
in the unity of the Holy Spirit,
one God, now and for ever.

POST-COMMUNION PRAYER

Almighty God,
you have given your only Son to be for us
both a sacrifice for sin
and also an example of godly life:
give us grace
that we may always most thankfully receive
these his inestimable gifts,
and also daily endeavour to follow
 the blessed steps of his most holy life;
through Jesus Christ our Lord.

THE FIRST SUNDAY OF LENT

COLLECT

Almighty God,
whose Son Jesus Christ fasted forty days in the wilderness,
and was tempted as we are, yet without sin:
Give us grace to discipline ourselves
    in obedience to your Spirit;
and, as you know our weakness,
so may we know your power to save;
through Jesus Christ your Son our Lord,
who is alive and reigns with you
in the unity of the Holy Spirit,
one God, now and for ever.

POST-COMMUNION PRAYER

Lord God,
you have renewed us with the living bread from heaven;
by it you nourish our faith,
increase our hope,
and strengthen our love:
teach us always to hunger for him
    who is the true and living bread,
and enable us to live by every word
    that proceeds from out of your mouth;
through Jesus Christ our Lord.

THE SECOND SUNDAY OF LENT

COLLECT

Almighty God,
you show to those who are in error the light of your truth,
that they may return to the way of righteousness:
grant to all those who are admitted
    into the fellowship of Christ's religion,

that they may reject those things
   that are contrary to their profession,
and follow all such things as are agreeable to the same;
through our Lord Jesus Christ,
who is alive and reigns with you
in the unity of the Holy Spirit,
one God, now and for ever.

POST-COMMUNION PRAYER

Almighty God,
you see that we have no power of ourselves to help
   ourselves:
keep us both outwardly in our bodies,
and inwardly in our souls;
that we may be defended from all adversities
   which may happen to the body,
and from all evil thoughts
   which may assault and hurt the soul;
through Jesus Christ our Lord.

THE THIRD SUNDAY OF LENT

COLLECT

Almighty God,
whose most dear Son went not up to joy
   but first he suffered pain,
and entered not into glory before he was crucified:
mercifully grant that we, walking in the way of the cross,
may find it none other than the way of life and peace;
through Jesus Christ your Son our Lord,
who is alive and reigns with you
in the unity of the Holy Spirit,
one God, now and for ever.

POST-COMMUNION PRAYER

Merciful Lord,
grant your people grace to withstand the temptations
    of the world, the flesh and the devil,
and with pure hearts and minds to follow you,
    the only God;
through Jesus Christ our Lord.

THE FOURTH SUNDAY OF LENT

COLLECT

Merciful Lord,
absolve your people from their offences,
that through your bountiful goodness
we may all be delivered from the chains of those sins
which by our frailty we have committed;
grant this, heavenly Father,
for Jesus Christ's sake, our blessed Lord and Saviour,
who is alive and reigns with you
in the unity of the Holy Spirit,
one God, now and for ever.

POST-COMMUNION PRAYER

Lord God,
whose blessed Son our Saviour
gave his back to the smiters
and did not hide his face from shame:
give us grace to endure the sufferings of this present time
with sure confidence in the glory that shall be revealed;
through Jesus Christ our Lord.

MOTHERING SUNDAY
(The Fourth Sunday of Lent)

COLLECT

God of compassion,
whose Son Jesus Christ, the child of Mary,
shared the life of a home in Nazareth,
and on the cross drew the whole human family to himself:
strengthen us in our daily living
that in joy and sorrow
we may know the power of your presence
  to bind together and to heal;
through Jesus Christ your Son our Lord,
who is alive and reigns with you
in the unity of the Holy Spirit,
one God, now and for ever.

POST-COMMUNION PRAYER

Loving God,
as a mother feeds her children at the breast
you feed us in this sacrament
  with the food and drink of eternal life:
help us who have tasted your goodness
to grow in grace within the household of faith;
through Jesus Christ our Lord.

THE FIFTH SUNDAY OF LENT

COLLECT

Most merciful God,
who by the death and resurrection of your Son Jesus Christ
delivered and saved the world:
grant that by faith in him who suffered on the cross
we may triumph in the power of his victory;
through Jesus Christ your Son our Lord,
who is alive and reigns with you
in the unity of the Holy Spirit,
one God, now and for ever.

POST-COMMUNION PRAYER

Lord Jesus Christ,
you have taught us
that what we do for the least of our brothers and sisters
we do also for you:
give us the will to be the servant of others
as you were the servant of all,
and gave up your life and died for us,
but are alive and reign, now and for ever.

_____ Holy Week _____

PALM SUNDAY

COLLECT

Almighty and everlasting God,
who in your tender love towards the human race
   sent your Son our Saviour Jesus Christ
to take upon him our flesh
and to suffer death upon the cross:
grant that we may follow the example
   of his patience and humility,
and also be made partakers of his resurrection;
through Jesus Christ your Son our Lord,
who is alive and reigns with you
in the unity of the Holy Spirit,
one God, now and for ever.

POST-COMMUNION PRAYER

Lord Jesus Christ,
you humbled yourself in taking the form of a servant,
and in obedience died on the cross for our salvation:
give us the mind to follow you
and to proclaim you as Lord and King,
to the glory of God the Father.

MONDAY TO WEDNESDAY
IN HOLY WEEK

COLLECT

Almighty and everlasting God,
who in your tender love towards the human race
    sent your Son our Saviour Jesus Christ
to take upon him our flesh
and to suffer death upon the cross:
grant that we may follow the example
    of his patience and humility,
and also be made partakers of his resurrection;
through Jesus Christ your Son our Lord,
who is alive and reigns with you
in the unity of the Holy Spirit,
one God, now and for ever.

POST-COMMUNION PRAYER

Lord Jesus Christ,
you humbled yourself in taking the form of a servant
and in obedience died on the cross for our salvation:
give us the mind to follow you
and to proclaim you as Lord and King,
to the glory of God the Father.

MAUNDY THURSDAY

COLLECT

God our Father,
you have invited us to share in the supper
which your Son gave to his Church
to proclaim his death until he comes:
may he nourish us by his presence,
and unite us in his love;

who is alive and reigns with you
in the unity of the Holy Spirit,
one God, now and for ever.

POST-COMMUNION PRAYER

Lord Jesus Christ,
we thank you that in this wonderful sacrament
you have given us the memorial of your passion:
grant us so to reverence the sacred mysteries
   of your body and blood
that we may know within ourselves
and show forth in our lives
the fruits of your redemption,
for you are alive and reign, now and for ever.

GOOD FRIDAY

COLLECT

Almighty Father,
look with mercy on this your family
for which our Lord Jesus Christ
   was content to be betrayed
    and given up into the hands of sinners
    and to suffer death upon the cross;
who is alive and glorified
   with you and the Holy Spirit,
one God, now and for ever.

POST-COMMUNION PRAYER

Most merciful God,
who by the death and resurrection of your Son Jesus Christ
delivered and saved the world:
grant that by faith in him who suffered on the cross
we may triumph in the power of his victory;
through Jesus Christ our Lord.

EASTER EVE

COLLECT

Grant, Lord,
that we who are baptized into the death
    of your Son our Saviour Jesus Christ
may continually put to death our evil desires
    and be buried with him;
that through the grave and gate of death
we may pass to our joyful resurrection;
through his merits , who died and was buried
    and rose again for us,
your Son Jesus Christ our Lord.

Easter

EASTER DAY

COLLECT

Lord of all life and power,
who through the mighty resurrection of your Son
overcame the old order of sin and death
to make all things new in him:
grant that we, being dead to sin
and alive to you in Jesus Christ,
may reign with him in glory;
to whom with you and the Holy Spirit
be praise and honour, glory and might,
now and in all eternity.

POST-COMMUNION PRAYER

God of Life,
who for our redemption gave your only-begotten Son
    to the death of the cross,
and by his glorious resurrection
have delivered us from the power of our enemy:
grant us so to die daily to sin,
that we may evermore live with him
    in the joy of his risen life;
through Jesus Christ our Lord.

THE SECOND SUNDAY OF EASTER

COLLECT

Almighty Father,
you have given your only Son to die for our sins
and to rise again for our justification:
grant us so to put away the leaven of malice and wickedness
that we may always serve you
in pureness of living and truth;
through the merits of your Son Jesus Christ our Lord,
who is alive and reigns with you
in the unity of the Holy Spirit,
one God, now and for ever.

POST-COMMUNION PRAYER

Lord God our Father,
through our Saviour Jesus Christ
you have assured your children of eternal life
and in baptism have made us one with him:
deliver us from the death of sin
and raise us to new life in your love,
in the fellowship of the Holy Spirit,
by the grace of our Lord Jesus Christ.

THE THIRD SUNDAY OF EASTER

COLLECT

Almighty Father,
who in your great mercy gladdened the disciples
    with the sight of the risen Lord:
give us such knowledge of his presence with us,
that we may be strengthened and sustained
    by his risen life
and serve you continually in righteousness and truth;

through Jesus Christ your Son our Lord,
who is alive and reigns with you
in the unity of the Holy Spirit,
one God, now and for ever.

POST-COMMUNION PRAYER

Living God,
your Son made himself known to his disciples
in the breaking of the bread:
open the eyes of our faith,
that we may see him in all his redeeming work;
who is alive and reigns, now and for ever.

THE FOURTH SUNDAY OF EASTER

COLLECT

Almighty God,
whose Son Jesus Christ is the resurrection and the life:
raise us, who trust in him,
from the death of sin to the life of righteousness,
that we may seek those things which are above,
where he reigns with you
in the unity of the Holy Spirit,
one God, now and for ever.

POST-COMMUNION PRAYER

Merciful Father,
you gave your Son Jesus Christ to be the good shepherd,
and in his love for us to lay down his life and rise again:
keep us always under his protection,
and give us grace to follow in his steps;
through Jesus Christ our Lord.

THE FIFTH SUNDAY OF EASTER

COLLECT

Almighty God,
who through your only-begotten Son Jesus Christ
have overcome death and opened to us the
    gate of everlasting life:
grant that, as by your grace going before us
    you put into our minds good desires,
so by your continual help
we may bring them to good effect;
through Jesus Christ our risen Lord,
who is alive and reigns with you
in the unity of the Holy Spirit,
one God, now and for ever.

POST-COMMUNION PRAYER

Eternal God,
whose Son Jesus Christ is the way, the truth and the life:
Grant us to walk in his way,
to rejoice in his truth,
and to share his risen life;
who is alive and reigns, now and for ever.

THE SIXTH SUNDAY OF EASTER

COLLECT

God our redeemer,
you have delivered us from the power of darkness
and brought us into the kingdom of your Son:
grant, that as by his death he has recalled us to life,
so by his continual presence in us he may raise us
    to eternal joy;

through Jesus Christ your Son our Lord,
who is alive and reigns with you
in the unity of the Holy Spirit,
one God, now and for ever.

POST-COMMUNION PRAYER

God our Father,
whose Son Jesus Christ gives us the water of eternal life:
may we thirst for you,
the spring of life and source of goodness,
through him who is alive and reigns, now and for ever.

ASCENSION DAY

COLLECT

Grant, we pray, almighty God,
that as we believe your only-begotten Son
    our Lord Jesus Christ
to have ascended into the heavens,
so we in heart and mind may also ascend
and with him continually dwell;
who is alive and reigns with you
in the unity of the Holy Spirit,
one God, now and for ever.

POST-COMMUNION PRAYER

God our Father,
you have raised our humanity in Christ
and have fed us with the bread of heaven:
mercifully grant that, nourished with such spiritual blessings,
we may set our hearts in the heavenly places;
through Jesus Christ our Lord.

THE SEVENTH SUNDAY OF EASTER

COLLECT

O God the King of Glory,
you have exalted your only Son Jesus Christ
with great triumph to your kingdom in heaven:
we beseech you, leave us not comfortless,
but send your Holy Spirit to strengthen us
and exalt us to the place
   where our Saviour Christ is gone before,
who is alive and reigns with you
in the unity of the Holy Spirit,
one God, now and for ever.

POST-COMMUNION PRAYER

Eternal God, giver of love and power,
your Son Jesus Christ has sent us into all the world
to preach the gospel of his kingdom:
confirm us in this mission,
and help us to live the good news we proclaim;
through Jesus Christ our Lord.

PENTECOST

COLLECT

God, who as at this time
taught the hearts of your faithful people
by sending to them the light of your Holy Spirit:
grant us by the same Spirit
to have a right judgement in all things
and evermore to rejoice in his holy comfort;
through the merits of Christ Jesus our Saviour,
who is alive and reigns with you
in the unity of the Holy Spirit,
one God, now and for ever.

POST-COMMUNION PRAYER

Faithful God,
who fulfilled the promises of Easter
by sending us your Holy Spirit
and opening to every race and nation
the way of life eternal:
open our lips by your Spirit,
that every tongue may tell of your glory;
through Jesus Christ our Lord.

_____Ordinary Time_____

PENTECOST WEEK
Monday to Saturday

COLLECT

O Lord, from whom all good things come:
grant to us your humble servants,
that by your holy inspiration
we may think those things that are good,
and by your merciful guiding may perform the same;
through our Lord Jesus Christ,
who is alive and reigns with you
in the unity of the Holy Spirit,
one God, now and for ever.

POST-COMMUNION PRAYER

Gracious God, lover of all,
in this sacrament
we are one family in Christ your Son,
one in the sharing of his body and blood
and one in the communion of the Spirit:
help us to grow in love for one another
and come to the full maturity of the Body of Christ.
We make our prayer through your Son our Saviour.

TRINITY SUNDAY

COLLECT

Almighty and everlasting God,
you have given us your servants grace,
by the confession of a true faith,
to acknowledge the glory of the eternal Trinity
and in the power of the divine majesty to worship the Unity:
keep us steadfast in this faith,
that we may evermore be defended from all adversities;
through Jesus Christ your Son our Lord,
who is alive and reigns with you
in the unity of the Holy Spirit,
one God, now and for ever.

POST-COMMUNION PRAYER

Almighty and eternal God,
you have revealed yourself as Father, Son and Holy Spirit,
and live and reign in the perfect unity of love:
hold us firm in this faith,
that we may know you in all your ways
and evermore rejoice in your eternal glory,
who are three Persons yet one God,
now and for ever.

CORPUS CHRISTI
*Day of Thanksgiving for the Holy Communion
Thursday after Trinity Sunday*

COLLECT

Lord Jesus Christ,
we thank you that in this wonderful sacrament
you have given us the memorial of your passion:
grant us so to reverence the sacred mysteries
  of your body and blood

195

that we may know within ourselves
and show forth in our lives
the fruits of your redemption;
for you are alive and reign with the Father
in the unity of the Holy Spirit,
one God, now and for ever.

POST-COMMUNION PRAYER

All praise to you, our God and Father,
for you have fed us with the bread of heaven
and quenched our thirst from the true vine:
hear our prayer that, being grafted into Christ,
we may grow together in unity
and feast with him in his kingdom;
through Jesus Christ our Lord.

THE FIRST SUNDAY AFTER TRINITY

COLLECT

O God,
the strength of all those who put their trust in you,
mercifully accept our prayers
and, because through the weakness of our mortal nature
we can do no good thing without you,
grant us the help of your grace,
that in the keeping of your commandments
we may please you both in will and deed;
through Jesus Christ your Son our Lord,
who is alive and reigns with you
in the unity of the Holy Spirit,
one God, now and for ever.

POST-COMMUNION PRAYER

Eternal Father,
we thank you for nourishing us
with these heavenly gifts:
may our communion strengthen us in faith,
build us up in hope
and make us grow in love;
for the sake of Jesus Christ our Lord.

THE SECOND SUNDAY AFTER TRINITY

COLLECT

Lord, you have taught us
that all our doings without love are nothing worth:
send your Holy Spirit
and pour into our hearts that most excellent gift of love,
the true bond of peace and of all virtues,
without which whoever lives is counted dead before you.
Grant this for your only Son Jesus Christ's sake,
who is alive and reigns with you
in the unity of the Holy Spirit,
one God, now and for ever.

POST-COMMUNION PRAYER

Loving Father,
we thank you for feeding us at the supper of your Son:
sustain us with your Spirit,
that we may serve you here on earth
until our joy is complete in heaven,
and we share in the eternal banquet
with Jesus Christ our Lord.

THE THIRD SUNDAY AFTER TRINITY

COLLECT

Almighty God,
you have broken the tyranny of sin
and have sent the Spirit of your Son into our hearts
    whereby we call you Father:
give us grace to dedicate our freedom to your service,
that we and all creation may be brought
    to the glorious liberty of the children of God;
through Jesus Christ your Son our Lord,
who is alive and reigns with you
in the unity of the Holy Spirit,
one God, now and for ever.

POST-COMMUNION PRAYER

O God, whose beauty is beyond our imagining
and whose power we cannot comprehend:
show us your glory as far as we can grasp it,
and shield us from knowing more than we can bear
until we may look upon you without fear;
through Jesus Christ our Saviour.

THE FOURTH SUNDAY AFTER TRINITY

COLLECT

O God the protector of all who trust in you,
without whom nothing is strong, nothing is holy:
increase and multiply upon us your mercy;
that with you as our ruler and guide
we may so pass through things temporal
that we lose not our hold on things eternal;
grant this, heavenly Father,
for our Lord Jesus Christ's sake,
who is alive and reigns with you
in the unity of the Holy Spirit,
one God, now and for ever.

POST-COMMUNION PRAYER

Eternal God,
comfort of the afflicted and healer of the broken,
you have fed us at the table of life and hope:
teach us the ways of gentleness and peace,
that all the world may acknowledge
the kingdom of your Son Jesus Christ our Lord.

THE FIFTH SUNDAY AFTER TRINITY

COLLECT

Almighty and everlasting God,
by whose Spirit the whole body of the Church
   is governed and sanctified:
hear our prayer which we offer for all your faithful people,
that in their vocation and ministry
they may serve you in holiness and truth
to the glory of your name;
through our Lord and Saviour Jesus Christ,
who is alive and reigns with you
in the unity of the Holy Spirit,
one God, now and for ever.

POST-COMMUNION PRAYER

Grant, O Lord, we beseech you,
that the course of this world may be so peaceably ordered
   by your governance,
that your Church may joyfully serve you
   in all godly quietness;
through Jesus Christ our Lord.

THE SIXTH SUNDAY AFTER TRINITY

COLLECT

Merciful God,
you have prepared for those who love you
such good things as pass our understanding:
pour into our hearts such love towards you
that we, loving you in all things and above all things,
may obtain your promises,
which exceed all that we can desire;
through Jesus Christ your Son our Lord,
who is alive and reigns with you
in the unity of the Holy Spirit,
one God, now and for ever.

POST-COMMUNION PRAYER

God of our pilgrimage,
you have led us to the living water:
refresh and sustain us
as we go forward on our journey,
in the name of Jesus Christ our Lord.

THE SEVENTH SUNDAY AFTER TRINITY

COLLECT

Lord of all power and might,
the author and giver of all good things:
graft in our hearts the love of your name,
increase in us true religion,
nourish us with all goodness,
and of your great mercy keep us in the same;
through Jesus Christ your Son our Lord,

who is alive and reigns with you
in the unity of the Holy Spirit,
one God, now and for ever.

POST-COMMUNION PRAYER

Lord God, whose Son is the true vine and the source of life,
ever giving himself that the world may live:
may we so receive within ourselves
    the power of his death and passion
that, in his saving cup,
    we may share his glory and be made perfect in his love;
for he is alive and reigns, now and for ever.

THE EIGHTH SUNDAY AFTER TRINITY

COLLECT

Almighty Lord and everlasting God,
we beseech you to direct, sanctify and govern
    both our hearts and bodies
in the ways of your laws
    and the works of your commandments;
that through your most mighty protection, both here and
    ever,
we may be preserved in body and soul;
through our Lord and Saviour Jesus Christ,
who is alive and reigns with you
in the unity of the Holy Spirit,
one God, now and for ever.

POST-COMMUNION PRAYER

Strengthen for service, Lord,
the hands that have taken holy things;
may the ears which have heard your word
    be deaf to clamour and dispute;

may the tongues which have sung your praise
    be free from deceit;
may the eyes which have seen the tokens of your love
    shine with the light of hope;
and may the bodies which have been fed with your body
    be refreshed with the fullness of your life;
glory to you for ever.

THE NINTH SUNDAY AFTER TRINITY

COLLECT

Almighty God,
who sent your Holy Spirit
to be the life and light of your Church:
open our hearts to the riches of his grace,
that we may bring forth the fruit of the Spirit
in love and joy and peace;
through Jesus Christ your Son our Lord,
who is alive and reigns with you
in the unity of the Holy Spirit,
one God, now and for ever.

POST-COMMUNION PRAYER

Holy Father,
who gathered us here around the table of your Son,
to share this meal with the whole household of God:
in that new world where you reveal the fullness of your peace,
gather people of every race and language
    to share in the eternal banquet
    of Jesus Christ our Lord.

THE TENTH SUNDAY AFTER TRINITY

COLLECT

Let your merciful ears, O Lord,
be open to the prayers of your humble servants;
and that they may obtain their petitions
make them to ask such things as shall please you;
through Jesus Christ your Son our Lord,
who is alive and reigns with you
in the unity of the Holy Spirit,
one God, now and for ever.

POST-COMMUNION PRAYER

God of our pilgrimage,
you have willed that the gate of mercy
should stand open for those who trust in you:
look upon us with your favour
that we who follow the path of your will
may never wander from the way of life;
through Jesus Christ our Lord.

THE ELEVENTH SUNDAY AFTER TRINITY

COLLECT

O God, you declare your almighty power
most chiefly in showing mercy and pity:
mercifully grant to us such a measure of your grace,
that we, running the way of your commandments,
may receive your gracious promises,
and be made partakers of your heavenly treasure;
through Jesus Christ your Son our Lord,
who is alive and reigns with you
in the unity of the Holy Spirit,
one God, now and for ever.

POST-COMMUNION PRAYER

Lord of all mercy,
we your faithful people have celebrated that one true sacrifice
    which takes away our sins and brings pardon and peace:
by our communion
keep us firm on the foundation of the gospel
and preserve us from all sin;
    through Jesus Christ our Lord.

THE TWELFTH SUNDAY AFTER TRINITY

COLLECT

Almighty and everlasting God,
you are always more ready to hear than we to pray
and to give more than either we desire or deserve:
pour down upon us the abundance of your mercy,
forgiving us those things of which our conscience is afraid
and giving us those good things
    which we are not worthy to ask
but through the merits and mediation
of Jesus Christ your Son our Lord,
who is alive and reigns with you
in the unity of the Holy Spirit,
one God, now and for ever.

POST-COMMUNION PRAYER

God of all mercy,
in this eucharist you have set aside our sins
and given us your healing:
grant that we who are made whole in Christ
may bring that healing to this broken world,
in the name of Jesus Christ our Lord.

THE THIRTEENTH SUNDAY AFTER TRINITY

COLLECT

Almighty God,
you called your Church to bear witness
that you were in Christ reconciling the world to yourself:
help us to proclaim the good news of your love,
that all who hear it may be drawn to you;
through him who was lifted up on the cross,
and reigns with you in the unity of the Holy Spirit,
one God, now and for ever.

POST-COMMUNION PRAYER

God our creator,
you feed your children with the true manna,
the living bread from heaven:
let this holy food sustain us through our earthly pilgrimage
until we come to that place
    where hunger and thirst are no more;
through Jesus Christ our Lord.

THE FOURTEENTH SUNDAY AFTER TRINITY

COLLECT

Almighty God,
whose only Son has opened for us
a new and living way into your presence:
give us pure hearts and steadfast wills
to worship you in spirit and in truth;
through Jesus Christ your Son our Lord,
who is alive and reigns with you
in the unity of the Holy Spirit,
one God, now and for ever.

POST-COMMUNION PRAYER

Lord God, the source of truth and love,
keep us faithful to the apostles' teaching and fellowship,
united in prayer and the breaking of bread,
and one in joy and simplicity of heart,
in Jesus Christ our Lord.

THE FIFTEENTH SUNDAY
AFTER TRINITY

COLLECT

O God,
who in generous mercy sent the Holy Spirit
    upon your Church in the burning fire of your love:
grant that your people may be fervent
    in the fellowship of the gospel,
that, always abiding in you,
they may be found steadfast in faith and active in service;
through Jesus Christ your Son our Lord,
who is alive and reigns with you
in the unity of the Holy Spirit,
one God, now and for ever.

POST-COMMUNION PRAYER

Keep O Lord, your Church
    with your perpetual mercy;
and, because without you our human frailty cannot but fall,
keep us ever by your help from all things hurtful
and lead us to all things profitable to our salvation;
through Jesus Christ our Lord.

THE SIXTEENTH SUNDAY AFTER TRINITY

COLLECT

O Lord, we beseech you mercifully to hear the prayers
    of your people who call upon you;
and grant that they may both perceive and know
    what things they ought to do,
and also may have grace and power
    faithfully to fulfil them;
through Jesus Christ your Son our Lord,
who is alive and reigns with you
in the unity of the Holy Spirit,
one God, now and for ever.

POST-COMMUNION PRAYER

Almighty God,
you have taught us through your Son
that love is the fulfilling of the law:
grant that we may love you with our whole heart
and our neighbours as ourselves;
through Jesus Christ our Lord.

THE SEVENTEENTH SUNDAY AFTER TRINITY

COLLECT

Almighty God, you have made us for yourself,
and our hearts are restless till they find their rest in you:
pour your love into our hearts and draw us to yourself,
and so bring us at the last to your heavenly city
where we shall see you face to face;
through Jesus Christ your Son our Lord,
who is alive and reigns with you
in the unity of the Holy Spirit,
one God, now and for ever.

POST-COMMUNION PRAYER

Lord, we pray that your grace
   may always precede and follow us
and make us continually to be given to all good works;
through Jesus Christ our Lord.

THE EIGHTEENTH SUNDAY
AFTER TRINITY

COLLECT

Almighty and everlasting God,
increase in us your gift of faith;
that, forsaking what lies behind
and reaching out to that which is before,
we may run the way of your commandments
and win the crown of everlasting joy;
through Jesus Christ your Son our Lord,
who is alive and reigns with you
in the unity of the Holy Spirit,
one God, now and for ever.

POST-COMMUNION PRAYER

We praise and thank you, O Christ, for this sacred feast:
for here we receive you,
here the memory of your passion is renewed,
our minds are filled with grace,
and here a pledge of future glory is given,
when we shall feast at that table where you reign
with all your saints for ever.

THE NINETEENTH SUNDAY
AFTER TRINITY

COLLECT

O God, forasmuch as without you
we are not able to please you;
mercifully grant that your Holy Spirit
may in all things direct and rule our hearts;
through Jesus Christ your Son our Lord,
who is alive and reigns with you
in the unity of the Holy Spirit,
one God, now and for ever.

POST-COMMUNION PRAYER

Holy and blessed God,
you have fed us with the body and blood of your Son
and filled us with your Holy Spirit:
may we honour you not only with our lips,
but in lives dedicated to the service of Jesus Christ our Lord.

THE TWENTIETH SUNDAY
AFTER TRINITY

COLLECT

God, the giver of life,
whose Holy Spirit wells up within your Church:
by the Spirit's gifts equip us to live the gospel of Christ
    and make us eager to do your will,
that we may share with the whole creation
    the joys of eternal life;
through Jesus Christ your Son our Lord,
who is alive and reigns with you
in the unity of the Holy Spirit,
one God, now and for ever.

POST-COMMUNION PRAYER

God our Father,
whose Son, the light unfailing,
has come from heaven to deliver the world
    from the darkness of ignorance:
let these holy mysteries open the eyes of our understanding
that we may know the way of life,
and walk in it without stumbling;
through Jesus Christ our Lord.

THE TWENTY-FIRST SUNDAY
AFTER TRINITY

COLLECT

Grant, we beseech you, merciful Lord,
to your faithful people pardon and peace;
that they may be cleansed from all their sins
and serve you with a quiet mind;
through Jesus Christ your Son our Lord,
who is alive and reigns with you
in the unity of the Holy Spirit,
one God, now and for ever.

POST-COMMUNION PRAYER

Father of light,
in whom is no change or shadow of turning,
you give us every good and perfect gift
and have brought us to birth by your word of truth:
may we be a living sign of that kingdom
where your whole creation will be made perfect
    in Jesus Christ our Lord.

LAST SUNDAY AFTER TRINITY

See also Dedication Festival, page 212.

COLLECT

Blessed Lord,
who caused all holy scriptures
    to be written for our learning:
help us so to hear them,
to read, mark, learn and inwardly digest them,
that, through patience and the comfort of your holy word,
we may embrace and for ever hold fast
    the hope of everlasting life,
which you have given us in our Saviour Jesus Christ,
who is alive and reigns with you
in the unity of the Holy Spirit,
one God, now and for ever.

POST-COMMUNION PRAYER

God of all grace,
your Son Jesus Christ fed the hungry
with the bread of his life
and the word of his kingdom:
renew your people with your heavenly grace,
and in all our weakness
sustain us by your true and living bread;
who is alive and reigns, now and for ever.

DEDICATION FESTIVAL

First Sunday in October or Last Sunday after Trinity

COLLECT

Almighty God,
to whose glory we celebrate the dedication
   of this house of prayer:
we praise you for the many blesssings
you have given to those who worship you here:
and we pray that all who seek you in this place
   may find you,
and, being filled with the Holy Spirit,
may become a living temple acceptable to you;
through Jesus Christ your Son our Lord,
who is alive and reigns with you
in the unity of the Holy Spirit,
one God, now and for ever.

POST-COMMUNION PRAYER

Father in heaven,
whose Church on earth is a sign of your heavenly peace,
an image of the new and eternal Jerusalem:
grant to us in the days of our pilgrimage
that, fed with the living bread from heaven,
and united in the body of your Son,
we may be the temple of your presence,
the place of your glory on earth,
and a sign of your peace in the world;
through Jesus Christ our Lord.

ALL SAINTS

1 November or the Fourth Sunday before Advent

COLLECT

Almighty God,
you have knit together your elect
in one communion and fellowship
   in the mystical body of your Son Christ our Lord:
grant us grace so to follow your blessèd saints
in all virtuous and godly living
that we may come to those inexpressible joys
that you have prepared for those who truly love you;
through Jesus Christ your Son our Lord,
who is alive and reigns with you
in the unity of the Holy Spirit,
one God, now and for ever.

POST-COMMUNION PRAYER

God, the source of all holiness
   and giver of all good things:
may we who have shared at this table
   as strangers and pilgrims here on earth
be welcomed with all your saints
   to the heavenly feast on the day of your kingdom;
through Jesus Christ our Lord.

THE FOURTH SUNDAY BEFORE ADVENT

For use when All Saints' Day is observed on a weekday.

COLLECT

Almighty and eternal God,
you have kindled the flame of love
   in the hearts of the saints:
grant to us the same faith and power of love,
that, as we rejoice in their triumphs,
we may be sustained by their example and fellowship;
through Jesus Christ your Son our Lord,
who is alive and reigns with you
in the unity of the Holy Spirit,
one God, now and for ever.

POST-COMMUNION PRAYER

Lord of heaven,
in this eucharist you have brought us near
   to an innumerable company of angels
   and to the spirits of the saints made perfect:
as in this food of our earthly pilgrimage
   we have shared their fellowship,
so may we come to share the fullness of joy in heaven;
through Jesus Christ our Lord.

THE THIRD SUNDAY BEFORE ADVENT

COLLECT

Almighty Father,
whose will is to restore all things
in your beloved Son, the King of all:
govern the hearts and minds of those in authority,
and bring the families of the nations,
divided and torn apart by the ravages of sin,

to be subject to his just and gentle rule;
who is alive and reigns with you
in the unity of the Holy Spirit,
one God, now and for ever.

POST-COMMUNION PRAYER

God of peace,
whose Son Jesus Christ proclaimed the kingdom
and restored the broken to wholeness of life:
look with compassion on the anguish of the world,
and by your healing power
make whole both people and nations;
through our Lord and Saviour Jesus Christ.

THE SECOND SUNDAY BEFORE ADVENT

COLLECT

Heavenly Father, whose blessed Son was revealed
    to destroy the works of the devil
and to make us the children of God and heirs of eternal life:
grant that we, having this hope,
may purify ourselves even as he is pure;
that when he shall appear in power and great glory
we may be made like him
    in his eternal and glorious kingdom;
where he is alive and reigns with you
in the unity of the Holy Spirit,
one God, now and for ever.

POST-COMMUNION PRAYER

Gracious Lord,
in this holy sacrament you give substance to our hope:
bring us at the last to that fullness of life for which we long;
through Jesus Christ our Saviour.

CHRIST THE KING
The Sunday before Advent

COLLECT

Eternal Father,
whose Son Jesus Christ ascended to the throne of heaven
   that he might rule over all things as Lord and King:
keep the Church in the unity of the Spirit
and in the bond of peace,
and bring the whole created order to worship at his feet;
who is alive and reigns with you
in the unity of the Holy Spirit,
one God, now and for ever.

POST-COMMUNION PRAYER

Stir up, O Lord,
the wills of your faithful people;
that they, plenteously bringing forth the fruit of good works,
may by you be plenteously rewarded;
through Jesus Christ our Lord.

Holy Days

_____ Holy Days _____

*Full provision is not made here for most lesser festivals. The
provision for the Common of Saints (pages 251–8) may be
used, together with the authorized collects and other material from
the* Calendar, Lectionary and Collects.

THE NAMING AND CIRCUMCISION
OF JESUS
1 January

COLLECT

Almighty God,
whose blessed Son was circumcised
in obedience to the law for our sake
and given the Name that is above every name:
give us grace faithfully to bear his Name,
to worship him in the freedom of the Spirit,
and to proclaim him as the Saviour of the world;
who is alive and reigns with you
in the unity of the Holy Spirit,
one God, now and for ever.

POST-COMMUNION PRAYER

Eternal God,
whose incarnate Son was given the name of Saviour:
grant that we who have shared
    in this sacrament of our salvation
may live out our years in the power
    of the name above all other names,
Jesus Christ our Lord.

THE CONVERSION OF SAINT PAUL
25 January

COLLECT

Almighty God,
who caused the light of the gospel
to shine throughout the world
through the preaching of your servant Saint Paul:
grant that we who celebrate his wonderful conversion
may follow him in bearing witness to your truth;
through Jesus Christ your Son our Lord,
who is alive and reigns with you
in the unity of the Holy Spirit,
one God, now and for ever.

POST-COMMUNION PRAYER

Almighty God,
who on the day of Pentecost
sent your Holy Spirit to the apostles
with the wind from heaven and in tongues of flame,
filling them with joy and boldness to preach the gospel:
by the power of the same Spirit
strengthen us to witness to your truth
and to draw everyone to the fire of your love;
through Jesus Christ our Lord.

or

Lord God, the source of truth and love,
keep us faithful to the apostles' teaching and fellowship,
united in prayer and the breaking of bread,
and one in joy and simplicity of heart,
in Jesus Christ our Lord.

THE PRESENTATION OF CHRIST IN THE TEMPLE (CANDLEMAS)
2 February
or the Sunday nearest 31 January

See page 172.

TIMOTHY AND TITUS
26 January

COLLECT

Heavenly Father,
who sent your apostle Paul to preach the gospel,
and gave him Timothy and Titus to be his companions
    in faith:
grant that our fellowship in the Holy Spirit
may bear witness to the name of Jesus,
who is alive and reigns with you
in the unity of the Holy Spirit,
one God, now and for ever.

POST-COMMUNION PRAYER

Holy Father,
who gathered us here around the table of your Son
to share this meal with the whole household of God:
in that new world where you reveal
    the fullness of your peace,
gather people of every race and language,
to share with Timothy and Titus and all your saints
in the eternal banquet of Jesus Christ our Lord.

SAINT JOSEPH OF NAZARETH
19 March

COLLECT

God our Father,
who from the family of your servant David
raised up Joseph the carpenter
to be the guardian of your incarnate Son
and husband of the Blessed Virgin Mary:
give us grace to follow him
in faithful obedience to your commands;
through the same your Son Jesus Christ our Lord,
who is alive and reigns with you
in the unity of the Holy Spirit,
one God, now and for ever.

POST-COMMUNION PRAYER

Heavenly Father,
whose Son grew in wisdom and stature
in the home of Joseph the carpenter of Nazareth
and on the wood of the cross perfected the work
    of the world's salvation:
help us, strengthened by the sacrament of his passion,
to count the wisdom of the world as foolishness,
and to walk with him in simplicity and trust;
through Jesus Christ our Lord.

THE ANNUNCIATION OF OUR LORD
25 March

COLLECT

We beseech you, O Lord,
pour your grace into our hearts,
that as we have known the incarnation
    of your Son Jesus Christ

by the message of an angel,
so by his cross and passion
we may be brought to the glory of his resurrection;
who is alive and reigns with you
in the unity of the Holy Spirit,
one God, now and for ever.

POST-COMMUNION PRAYER

God Most High,
whose handmaid bore the Word made flesh:
we thank you that in this sacrament of our redemption
you visit us with your Holy Spirit
and overshadow us by your power,
strengthen us to walk with Mary the joyful path of obedience
and so bring forth the fruits of holiness;
through Jesus Christ our Lord.

SAINT GEORGE THE MARTYR
23 April

COLLECT

God of hosts,
who so kindled the flame of love
in the heart of your servant George
that he bore witness to the risen Lord
by his life and by his death:
give us the same faith and power of love
that we who rejoice in his triumphs
may come to share with him the fullness of the resurrection;
through Jesus Christ your Son our Lord,
who is alive and reigns with you
in the unity of the Holy Spirit,
one God, now and for ever.

POST-COMMUNION PRAYER

Eternal God,
who gave us this holy meal
in which we have celebrated the glory of the cross
and the victory of your martyr George:
by our communion with Christ
in his saving death and resurrection,
give us with all your saints the courage to conquer evil
and so to share in the fruit of the tree of life;
through Jesus Christ our Lord.

SAINT MARK THE EVANGELIST
25 April

COLLECT

Almighty God,
who enlightened your holy Church
through the inspired witness
    of your evangelist Saint Mark:
grant that we, being firmly grounded
    in the truth of the gospel,
may be faithful to its teaching both in word and deed;
through Jesus Christ your Son our Lord,
who is alive and reigns with you
in the unity of the Holy Spirit,
one God, now and for ever.

POST-COMMUNION PRAYER

Almighty God,
who on the day of Pentecost
sent your Holy Spirit to the apostles
with the wind from heaven and in tongues of flame,
filling them with joy and boldness to preach the gospel:
by the power of the same Spirit
strengthen us to witness to your truth
and to draw everyone to the fire of your love;
through Jesus Christ our Lord.

or

Lord God, the source of truth and love,
keep us faithful to the apostles' teaching and fellowship,
united in prayer and the breaking of bread,
and one in joy and simplicity of heart,
in Jesus Christ our Lord.

SAINT PHILIP AND SAINT JAMES
THE APOSTLES
1 May

COLLECT

Almighty Father,
whom truly to know is eternal life:
teach us to know your Son Jesus Christ
as the way, the truth and the life;
that we may follow the steps
    of your holy apostles Philip and James
and walk steadfastly in the way that leads to your glory;
through Jesus Christ your Son our Lord,
who is alive and reigns with you
in the unity of the Holy Spirit,
one God, now and for ever.

POST-COMMUNION PRAYER

Almighty God,
who on the day of Pentecost
sent your Holy Spirit to the apostles
with the wind from heaven and in tongues of flame,
filling them with joy and boldness to preach the gospel:
by the power of the same Spirit
strengthen us to witness to your truth
and to draw everyone to the fire of your love;
through Jesus Christ our Lord.

or

225

Lord God, the source of truth and love,
keep us faithful to the apostles' teaching and fellowship,
united in prayer and the breaking of bread,
and one in joy and simplicity of heart,
in Jesus Christ our Lord.

ENGLISH SAINTS AND MARTYRS OF THE REFORMATION ERA
4 May

COLLECT

Merciful God,
who, when your Church was torn apart
    by the ravages of sin,
raised up men and women in this land
who witnessed to their faith with courage and constancy:
give to your Church that peace which is your will,
and grant that those who have been divided on earth
    may be reconciled in heaven,
and share together in the vision of your glory;
through Jesus Christ your Son our Lord,
who is alive and reigns with you
in the unity of the same Spirit,
one God, now and for ever.

POST-COMMUNION PRAYER

God, the source of all holiness
    and giver of all good things:
may we who have shared at this table
    as strangers and pilgrims here on earth
be welcomed with all your saints
    to the heavenly feast on the day of your kingdom;
through Jesus Christ our Lord.

SAINT MATTHIAS THE APOSTLE
14 May

COLLECT

Almighty God,
who in the place of the traitor Judas
chose your faithful servant Matthias
to be of the number of the Twelve:
preserve your Church from false apostles
and, by the ministry of faithful pastors and teachers,
keep us steadfast in your truth;
through Jesus Christ your Son our Lord,
who is alive and reigns with you
in the unity of the Holy Spirit,
one God, now and for ever.

POST-COMMUNION PRAYER

Almighty God,
who on the day of Pentecost
sent your Holy Spirit to the apostles
with the wind from heaven and in tongues of flame,
filling them with joy and boldness to preach the gospel:
by the power of the same Spirit
strengthen us to witness to your truth
and to draw everyone to the fire of your love;
through Jesus Christ our Lord.

or

Lord God, the source of truth and love,
keep us faithful to the apostles' teaching and fellowship,
united in prayer and the breaking of bread,
and one in joy and simplicity of heart,
in Jesus Christ our Lord.

THE VISIT OF THE BLESSED VIRGIN MARY TO ELIZABETH
31 May

COLLECT

Mighty God,
by whose grace Elizabeth rejoiced with Mary
and greeted her as the mother of the Lord:
look with favour on your lowly servants
that, with Mary, we may magnify your holy name
and rejoice to acclaim her Son our Saviour,
who is alive and reigns with you
in the unity of the Holy Spirit,
one God, now and for ever.

POST-COMMUNION PRAYER

Gracious God,
who gave joy to Elizabeth and Mary
as they recognized the signs of redemption
    at work within them:
help us, who have shared in the joy of this eucharist,
to know the Lord deep within us
and his love shining out in our lives,
that the world may rejoice in your salvation;
through Jesus Christ our Lord.

SAINT BARNABAS THE APOSTLE
11 June

COLLECT

Bountiful God, giver of all gifts,
who poured your Spirit upon your servant Barnabas
and gave him grace to encourage others:
help us, by his example,
to be generous in our judgements

and unselfish in our service;
through Jesus Christ your Son our Lord,
who is alive and reigns with you
in the unity of the Holy Spirit,
one God, now and for ever.

POST-COMMUNION PRAYER

Lord God, the source of truth and love,
keep us faithful to the apostles' teaching and fellowship,
united in prayer and the breaking of bread,
and one in joy and simplicity of heart,
in Jesus Christ our Lord.

or

Almighty God,
who on the day of Pentecost
sent your Holy Spirit to the apostles
with the wind from heaven and in tongues of flame,
filling them with joy and boldness to preach the gospel:
by the power of the same Spirit
strengthen us to witness to your truth
and to draw everyone to the fire of your love;
through Jesus Christ our Lord.

THE BIRTH OF SAINT JOHN
THE BAPTIST
24 June

COLLECT

Almighty God,
by whose providence your servant John the Baptist
was wonderfully born
and sent to prepare the way of your Son our Saviour
by the preaching of repentance:
lead us to repent according to his preaching

and, after his example, constantly to speak the truth,
boldly to rebuke vice, and patiently suffer for the truth's sake;
through Jesus Christ your Son our Lord,
who is alive and reigns with you
in the unity of the Holy Spirit,
one God, now and for ever.

POST-COMMUNION PRAYER

Merciful Lord,
whose prophet John the Baptist
proclaimed your Son as the Lamb of God
   who takes away the sin of the world:
grant that we who in this sacrament have known
   your forgiveness and your life-giving love
may ever tell of your mercy and your peace;
through Jesus Christ our Lord.

SAINT PETER AND SAINT PAUL
THE APOSTLES
29 June

COLLECT

Almighty God,
whose blessed apostles Peter and Paul
glorified you in their death as in their life:
grant that your Church,
inspired by their teaching and example,
and made one by your Spirit,
may ever stand firm upon the one foundation,
Jesus Christ your Son our Lord,
who is alive and reigns with you
in the unity of the Holy Spirit,
one God, now and for ever.

or (where St Peter is celebrated alone)

Almighty God,
who inspired your apostle Saint Peter
to confess Jesus as Christ and Son of the living God:
build up your Church upon this rock,
that in unity and peace it may proclaim one truth
and follow one Lord, your Son our Saviour Jesus Christ,
who is alive and reigns with you
in the unity of the Holy Spirit,
one God, now and for ever.

POST-COMMUNION PRAYER

Almighty God,
who on the day of Pentecost
sent your Holy Spirit to the apostles
with the wind from heaven and in tongues of flame,
filling them with joy and boldness to preach the gospel:
by the power of the same Spirit
strengthen us to witness to your truth
and to draw everyone to the fire of your love;
through Jesus Christ our Lord.

or

Lord God, the source of truth and love,
keep us faithful to the apostles' teaching and fellowship,
united in prayer and the breaking of bread,
and one in joy and simplicity of heart,
in Jesus Christ our Lord.

SAINT THOMAS THE APOSTLE
3 July

COLLECT

Almighty and eternal God,
who, for the firmer foundation of our faith,
allowed your holy apostle Thomas
    to doubt the resurrection of your Son
till word and sight convinced him:
grant to us, who have not seen, that we also may believe

and so confess Christ as our Lord and our God;
who is alive and reigns with you
in the unity of the Holy Spirit,
one God, now and for ever.

POST-COMMUNION PRAYER

Almighty God,
who on the day of Pentecost
sent your Holy Spirit to the apostles
with the wind from heaven and in tongues of flame,
filling them with joy and boldness to preach the gospel:
by the power of the same Spirit
strengthen us to witness to your truth
and to draw everyone to the fire of your love;
through Jesus Christ our Lord.

or

Lord God, the source of truth and love,
keep us faithful to the apostles' teaching and fellowship,
united in prayer and the breaking of bread,
and one in joy and simplicity of heart,
in Jesus Christ our Lord.

SAINT MARY MAGDALENE
22 July

COLLECT

Almighty God,
whose Son restored Mary Magdalene
    to health of mind and body
and called her to be a witness to his resurrection:
forgive our sins and heal us by your grace,
that we may serve you in the power of his risen life;
who is alive and reigns with you
in the unity of the Holy Spirit,
one God, now and for ever.

POST-COMMUNION PRAYER

God of life and love,
whose risen Son called Mary Magdalene by name
and sent her to tell of his resurrection to his apostles:
in your mercy, help us,
who have been united with him in this eucharist,
to proclaim the good news
    that he is alive and reigns, now and for ever.

SAINT JAMES THE APOSTLE
25 July

COLLECT

Merciful God,
whose holy apostle Saint James,
leaving his father and all that he had,
was obedient to the calling of your Son Jesus Christ
and followed him even to death:
help us, forsaking the false attractions of the world,
to be ready at all times to answer your call without delay;
through Jesus Christ your Son our Lord,
who is alive and reigns with you
in the unity of the Holy Spirit,
one God, now and for ever.

POST-COMMUNION PRAYER

Almighty God,
who on the day of Pentecost
sent your Holy Spirit to the apostles
with the wind from heaven and in tongues of flame,
filling them with joy and boldness to preach the gospel:
by the power of the same Spirit
strengthen us to witness to your truth
and to draw everyone to the fire of your love;
through Jesus Christ our Lord.

233

or

Lord God, the source of truth and love,
keep us faithful to the apostles' teaching and fellowship,
united in prayer and the breaking of bread,
and one in joy and simplicity of heart,
in Jesus Christ our Lord.

ANNE AND JOACHIM
26 July

COLLECT

Lord God of Israel,
who bestowed such grace on Anne and Joachim
that their daughter Mary grew up obedient to your word
and made ready to be the mother of your Son:
help us to commit ourselves in all things to your keeping
and grant us the salvation you promised to your people;
through Jesus Christ your Son our Lord,
who is alive and reigns with you
in the unity of the same Spirit,
one God, now and for ever.

POST-COMMUNION PRAYER

Father,
from whom every family in heaven and on earth
    takes its name,
your servants Anne and Joachim revealed your goodness
    in a life of tranquillity and service:
grant that we who have gathered in faith around this table
may like them know the love of Christ
    that surpasses knowledge
and be filled with all your fullness;
through Jesus Christ our Lord.

or

God, the source of all holiness
    and giver of all good things:

may we who have shared at this table
    as strangers and pilgrims here on earth
be welcomed with all your saints
    to the heavenly feast on the day of your kingdom;
through Jesus Christ our Lord.

MARY, MARTHA AND LAZARUS
29 July

COLLECT

God our Father,
whose Son enjoyed the love of his friends,
    Mary, Martha and Lazarus,
in learning, argument and hospitality:
may we so rejoice in your love
that the world may come to know
    the depths of your wisdom, the wonder of your compassion
    and your power to bring life out of death;
through the merits of Jesus Christ,
our friend and brother,
who is alive and reigns with you
in the unity of the Holy Spirit,
one God, now and for ever.

POST-COMMUNION PRAYER

Father,
from whom every family in heaven and on earth
    takes its name,
your servants Mary, Martha and Lazarus revealed your
    goodness in a life of tranquillity and service:
grant that we who have gathered in faith around this table
may like them know the love of Christ
    that surpasses knowledge
and be filled with all your fullness;
through Jesus Christ our Lord.

or

God, the source of all holiness . . . (*from page 234*)

THE TRANSFIGURATION OF OUR LORD
6 August

COLLECT

Father in heaven,
whose Son Jesus Christ was wonderfully transfigured
before chosen witnesses upon the holy mountain,
and spoke of the exodus he would accomplish at Jerusalem:
give us strength so to hear his voice and bear our cross
that in the world to come we may see him as he is;
who is alive and reigns with you
in the unity of the Holy Spirit,
one God, now and for ever.

POST-COMMUNION PRAYER

Holy God,
we see your glory in the face of Jesus Christ:
may we who are partakers at his table
reflect his life in word and deed,
that all the world may know
  his power to change and save.
This we ask through Jesus Christ our Lord.

THE BLESSED VIRGIN MARY
15 August or (for pastoral reasons) 8 September

COLLECT

Almighty God,
who looked upon the lowliness of the Blessed Virgin Mary
and chose her to be the mother of your only Son:
grant that we who are redeemed by his blood
may share with her in the glory of your eternal kingdom;
through Jesus Christ your Son our Lord,
who is alive and reigns with you
in the unity of the Holy Spirit,
one God, now and for ever.

POST-COMMUNION PRAYER

God Most High,
whose handmaid bore the Word made flesh:
we thank you that in this sacrament of our redemption
you visit us with your Holy Spirit
and overshadow us with your power;
strengthen us to walk with Mary the joyful path of obedience
and so to bring forth the fruits of holiness;
through Jesus Christ our Lord.

SAINT BARTHOLOMEW THE APOSTLE
24 August

COLLECT

Almighty and everlasting God,
who gave to your apostle Bartholomew grace
    truly to believe and to preach your word:
grant that your Church
may love that word which he believed
and may faithfully preach and receive the same;
through Jesus Christ your Son our Lord,
who is alive and reigns with you
in the unity of the Holy Spirit,
one God, now and for ever.

POST-COMMUNION PRAYER

Almighty God,
who on the day of Pentecost
sent your Holy Spirit to the apostles
with the wind from heaven and in tongues of flame,
filling them with joy and boldness to preach the gospel:
by the power of the same Spirit
strengthen us to witness to your truth
and to draw everyone to the fire of your love;
through Jesus Christ our Lord.

or

Lord God, the source of truth and love,
keep us faithful to the apostles' teaching and fellowship,
united in prayer and the breaking of bread,
and one in joy and simplicity of heart,
in Jesus Christ our Lord.

THE BEHEADING OF SAINT JOHN THE BAPTIST
29 August

COLLECT

Almighty God,
who called your servant John the Baptist
to be the forerunner of your Son in birth and death:
strengthen us by your grace
that, as he suffered for the truth,
so we may boldly resist corruption and vice
and receive with him the unfading crown of glory;
through Jesus Christ your Son our Lord,
who is alive and reigns with you
in the unity of the Holy Spirit,
one God, now and for ever.

POST-COMMUNION PRAYER

Merciful Lord,
whose prophet John the Baptist
proclaimed your Son as the Lamb of God
    who takes away the sin of the world:
grant that we who in this sacrament have known
    your forgiveness and your life-giving love
may ever tell of your mercy and your peace;
through Jesus Christ our Lord.

THE BIRTH OF THE BLESSED
VIRGIN MARY
8 September

See also the Common of the Blessed Virgin Mary, page 251.

COLLECT

Almighty and everlasting God,
who stooped to raise fallen humanity
through the child-bearing of blessed Mary:
grant that we, who have seen your glory
   revealed in our human nature
and your love made perfect in our weakness,
may daily be renewed in your image
and conformed to the pattern of your Son
Jesus Christ our Lord,
who is alive and reigns with you
in the unity of the Holy Spirit,
one God, now and for ever.

POST-COMMUNION PRAYER

God Most High,
whose handmaid bore the Word made flesh:
we thank you that in this sacrament of our redemption
you visit us with you Holy Spirit
and overshadow us with your power;
strengthen us to walk with Mary the joyful path of obedience
and so to bring forth the fruits of holiness;
through Jesus Christ our Lord.

HOLY CROSS DAY
14 September

COLLECT

Almighty God,
who in the passion of your blessed Son
made an instrument of painful death
to be for us the means of life and peace:
grant us so to glory in the cross of Christ
that we may gladly suffer for his sake;
who is alive and reigns with you
in the unity of the Holy Spirit,
one God, now and for ever.

POST-COMMUNION PRAYER

Faithful God,
whose Son bore our sins in his body on the tree
and gave us this sacrament to show forth his death
    until he comes:
give us grace to glory in the cross of our Lord Jesus Christ,
for he is our salvation, our life and our hope,
who reigns as Lord, now and for ever.

SAINT MATTHEW
THE APOSTLE AND EVANGELIST
21 September

COLLECT

O Almighty God,
whose blessed Son called Matthew the tax-collector
to be an apostle and evangelist:
give us grace to forsake the selfish pursuit of gain
    and the possessive love of riches
that we may follow in the way of your Son Jesus Christ,
who is alive and reigns with you
in the unity of the Holy Spirit,
one God, now and for ever.

POST-COMMUNION PRAYER

Almighty God,
who on the day of Pentecost
sent your Holy Spirit to the apostles
with the wind from heaven and in tongues of flame,
filling them with joy and boldness to preach the gospel:
by the power of the same Spirit
strengthen us to witness to your truth
and to draw everyone to the fire of your love;
through Jesus Christ our Lord.

or

Lord God, the source of truth and love,
keep us faithful to the apostles' teaching and fellowship,
united in prayer and the breaking of bread,
and one in joy and simplicity of heart,
in Jesus Christ our Lord.

SAINT MICHAEL AND ALL ANGELS
29 September

COLLECT

Everlasting God,
you have ordained and constituted the ministries
    of angels and mortals in a wonderful order:
grant that as your holy angels always serve you in heaven,
so, at your command, they may help and defend us on earth;
through Jesus Christ your Son our Lord,
who is alive and reigns with you
in the unity of the Holy Spirit,
one God, now and for ever.

POST-COMMUNION PRAYER

Lord of heaven,
in this eucharist you have brought us near
    to an innumerable company of angels
    and to the spirits of the saints made perfect:

241

as in this food of our earthly pilgrimage
  we have shared their fellowship,
so may we come to their joy in heaven;
through Jesus Christ our Lord.

SAINT LUKE THE EVANGELIST
18 October

COLLECT

Almighty God,
you called Luke the physician,
whose praise is in the gospel,
to be an evangelist and physician of the soul:
by the grace of the Spirit
and through the wholesome medicine of the gospel,
give your Church the same love and power to heal;
through Jesus Christ your Son our Lord,
who is alive and reigns with you
in the unity of the Holy Spirit,
one God, now and for ever.

POST-COMMUNION PRAYER

Almighty God,
who on the day of Pentecost
sent your Holy Spirit to the apostles
with the wind from heaven and in tongues of flame,
filling them with joy and boldness to preach the gospel:
by the power of the same Spirit
strengthen us to witness to your truth
and to draw everyone to the fire of your love;
through Jesus Christ our Lord.

or

Lord God, the source of truth and love,
keep us faithful to the apostles' teaching and fellowship,
united in prayer and the breaking of bread,
and one in joy and simplicity of heart,
in Jesus Christ our Lord.

SAINT SIMON AND SAINT JUDE
THE APOSTLES
28 October

COLLECT

Almighty God,
who built your Church upon the foundation
   of the apostles and prophets,
with Jesus Christ himself as the chief corner-stone:
so join us together in unity of spirit by their doctrine,
that we may be made a holy temple acceptable to you;
through Jesus Christ your Son our Lord,
who is alive and reigns with you
in the unity of the Holy Spirit,
one God, now and for ever.

POST-COMMUNION PRAYER

Almighty God,
who on the day of Pentecost
sent your Holy Spirit to the apostles
with the wind from heaven and in tongues of flame,
filling them with joy and boldness to preach the gospel:
by the power of the same Spirit
strengthen us to witness to your truth
and to draw everyone to the fire of your love;
through Jesus Christ our Lord.

or

Lord God, the source of truth and love,
keep us faithful to the apostles' teaching and fellowship,
united in prayer and the breaking of bread,
and one in joy and simplicity of heart,
in Jesus Christ our Lord.

ALL SAINTS
1 November or Fourth Sunday before Advent

See page 213.

COMMEMORATION OF THE FAITHFUL DEPARTED (ALL SOULS' DAY)
2 November

COLLECT

Eternal God, our Maker and Redeemer,
grant us, with all the faithful departed,
the sure benefits of your Son's saving passion
    and glorious resurrection,
that, in the last day,
when you gather up all things in Christ,
we may with them enjoy the fullness of your promises;
through Jesus Christ your Son our Lord,
who is alive and reigns with you
in the unity of the Holy Spirit,
one God, now and for ever.

POST-COMMUNION PRAYER

God of love, may the death and resurrection of Christ
which we have celebrated in this eucharist
bring us, with all the faithful departed,
into the peace of your eternal home.
We ask this in the name of Jesus Christ,
our rock and our salvation,
to whom be glory for time and for eternity.

THE SAINTS AND MARTYRS
OF ENGLAND
8 November

COLLECT

God, whom the glorious company of the redeemed adore,
assembled from all times and places of your dominion:
we praise you for the saints of our own land
and for the many lamps their holiness has lit;
and we pray that we also may be numbered at last
with those who have done your will
   and declared your righteousness;
through Jesus Christ your Son our Lord,
who is alive and reigns with you
in the unity of the Holy Spirit,
one God, now and for ever.

POST-COMMUNION PRAYER

God, the source of all holiness
   and giver of all good things:
may we who have shared at this table
   as strangers and pilgrims here on earth
be welcomed with all your saints
   to the heavenly feast on the day of your kingdom;
through Jesus Christ our Lord.

SAINT ANDREW THE APOSTLE
30 November

COLLECT

Almighty God,
who gave such grace to your apostle Saint Andrew
that he readily obeyed the call of your Son Jesus Christ
   and brought his brother with him:
call us by your holy Word,
and give us grace to follow you without delay

245

and to tell the good news of your kingdom;
through Jesus Christ your Son our Lord,
who is alive and reigns with you
in the unity of the Holy Spirit,
one God, now and for ever.

POST-COMMUNION PRAYER

Almighty God,
who on the day of Pentecost
sent your Holy Spirit to the apostles
with the wind from heaven and in tongues of flame,
filling them with joy and boldness to preach the gospel:
by the power of the same Spirit
strengthen us to witness to your truth
and to draw everyone to the fire of your love;
through Jesus Christ our Lord.

or

Lord God, the source of truth and love,
keep us faithful to the apostles' teaching and fellowship,
united in prayer and the breaking of bread,
and one in joy and simplicity of heart,
in Jesus Christ our Lord.

SAINT STEPHEN THE FIRST MARTYR
26 December

COLLECT

Gracious Father,
who gave the first martyr Stephen
grace to pray for those who took up stones against him:
grant that in all our sufferings for the truth
we may learn to love even our enemies
and to seek forgiveness for those who desire our hurt,
looking up to heaven to him who was crucified for us,
Jesus Christ, our Mediator and Advocate,
who is alive and reigns with you
in the unity of the Holy Spirit,
one God, now and for ever.

POST-COMMUNION PRAYER

Merciful Lord,
we thank you for the signs of your mercy
revealed in birth and in death:
save us by the coming of your Son,
and give us joy in honouring Stephen,
first martyr of the new Israel;
through Jesus Christ our Lord.

SAINT JOHN THE EVANGELIST
27 December

COLLECT

Merciful Lord,
cast your bright beams of light upon the Church:
that, being enlightened by the teaching
    of your blessed apostle and evangelist Saint John,
we may so walk in the light of your truth
that we may at last attain to the light of everlasting life;
through Jesus Christ
your incarnate Son our Lord,
who is alive and reigns with you
in the unity of the Holy Spirit,
one God, now and for ever.

POST-COMMUNION PRAYER

Grant, O Lord, we pray,
that the Word made flesh
proclaimed by your apostle John
may, by the celebration of these holy mysteries,
ever abide and live within us;
through Jesus Christ our Lord.

THE HOLY INNOCENTS
28 December

COLLECT

Heavenly Father,
whose children suffered at the hands of Herod,
though they had done no wrong:
by the suffering of your Son
and by the innocence of our lives
frustrate all evil designs
and establish your reign of justice and peace;
through Jesus Christ your Son our Lord,
who is alive and reigns with you
in the unity of the Holy Spirit,
one God, now and for ever.

POST-COMMUNION PRAYER

Lord Jesus Christ,
in your humility you have stooped to share our human life
with the most defenceless of your children:
may we who have received these gifts of your passion
rejoice in celebrating the witness of the holy innocents
    to the purity of your sacrifice
    made once for all upon the cross;
for you are alive and reign, now and for ever.

DEDICATION FESTIVAL

See page 212.

Common of Saints

Common of Saints

THE BLESSED VIRGIN MARY

COLLECT

Almighty and everlasting God,
who stooped to raise fallen humanity
through the child-bearing of blessed Mary;
grant that we, who have seen your glory
    revealed in our human nature
and your love made perfect in our weakness,
may daily be renewed in your image
and conformed to the pattern of your Son
Jesus Christ our Lord,
who is alive and reigns with you
in the unity of the Holy Spirit,
one God, now and for ever.

POST-COMMUNION PRAYER

God Most High,
whose handmaid bore the Word made flesh:
we thank you that in this sacrament of our redemption
you visit us with your Holy Spirit
and overshadow us with your power;
strengthen us to walk with Mary the joyful path of obedience
and so to bring forth the fruits of holiness;
through Jesus Christ our Lord.

APOSTLES AND EVANGELISTS

COLLECT

Almighty God,
who built your Church upon the foundation
   of the apostles and prophets,
with Jesus Christ himself as the chief corner-stone:
so join us together in unity of spirit by their doctrine,
that we may be made a holy temple acceptable to you;
through Jesus Christ your Son our Lord,
who is alive and reigns with you
in the unity of the Holy Spirit,
one God, now and for ever.

POST-COMMUNION PRAYER

Almighty God,
who on the day of Pentecost
sent your Holy Spirit to the apostles
with the wind from heaven and in tongues of flame,
filling them with joy and boldness to preach the gospel:
by the power of the same Spirit
strengthen us to witness to your truth
and to draw everyone to the fire of your love;
through Jesus Christ our Lord.

or

Lord God, the source of truth and love,
keep us faithful to the apostles' teaching and fellowship,
united in prayer and the breaking of bread,
and one in joy and simplicity of heart,
in Jesus Christ our Lord.

MARTYRS

COLLECT

Almighty God,
by whose grace and power your holy martyr N
triumphed over suffering and was faithful unto death:
strengthen us with your grace,
that we may endure reproach and persecution

and faithfully bear witness to the name
   of Jesus Christ your Son our Lord,
who is alive and reigns with you
in the unity of the Holy Spirit,
one God, now and for ever.

POST-COMMUNION PRAYER

Eternal God,
who gave us this holy meal
in which we have celebrated the glory of the cross
and the victory of your martyr *N*:
by our communion with Christ
in his saving death and resurrection,
give us with all your saints the courage to conquer evil
and so to share in the fruit of the tree of life;
through Jesus Christ our Lord.

or

God our Redeemer,
whose Church was strengthened
   by the blood of your martyr *N*:
so bind us, in life and death, to Christ's sacrifice
that our lives, broken and offered with his,
may carry his death and proclaim his resurrection in the world;
through Jesus Christ our Lord.

TEACHERS OF THE FAITH

COLLECT

Almighty God,
who enlightened your Church
   by the teaching of your servant *N*:
enrich it evermore with your heavenly grace
and raise up faithful witnesses
who, by their life and teaching,
may proclaim the truth of your salvation;
through Jesus Christ your Son our Lord,
who is alive and reigns with you
in the unity of the Holy Spirit,
one God, now and for ever.

POST-COMMUNION PRAYER

God of truth,
whose Wisdom set her table
and invited us to eat the bread
    and drink the wine of the kingdom:
help us to lay aside all foolishness
and to live and walk in the way of insight,
that we may come with N
    to the eternal feast of heaven;
through Jesus Christ our Lord.

BISHOPS AND OTHER PASTORS

COLLECT

Eternal God,
you called N to proclaim your glory
    in a life of prayer and pastoral zeal:
keep the leaders of your Church faithful
and bless your people through their ministry,
that the Church may grow into the full stature
    of your Son Jesus Christ our Lord,
who is alive and reigns with you
in the unity of the Holy Spirit,
one God, now and for ever.

or (of a bishop)

Almighty God,
the light of the faithful and shepherd of souls,
who set your servant N to be a bishop in the Church,
to feed your sheep by the word of Christ
and to guide them by good example:
give us grace to keep the faith of the
Church and to follow in the footsteps
    of Jesus Christ your Son our Lord,
who is alive and reigns with you
in the unity of the Holy Spirit,
one God, now and for ever.

POST-COMMUNION PRAYER

God, shepherd of your people,

whose servant *N* revealed the loving service of Christ
    in his/her ministry as a pastor of your people:
by this eucharist in which we share
awaken within us the love of Christ
and keep us faithful to our Christian calling;
through him who laid down his life for us,
but is alive and reigns with you, now and for ever.

RELIGIOUS

COLLECT

Almighty God,
by whose grace *N*, kindled with the fire of your love,
became a burning and shining light in the Church:
inflame us with the same spirit of discipline and love,
that we may ever walk before you as children of light;
through Jesus Christ your Son our Lord,
who is alive and reigns with you
in the unity of the Holy Spirit,
one God, now and for ever.

POST-COMMUNION PRAYER

Merciful God,
who gave such grace to your servant *N*
that he/she served you with singleness of heart
and loved you above all things:
help us, whose communion with you
    has been renewed in this sacrament,
to forsake all that holds us back from following Christ
and to grow into his likeness from glory to glory;
through Jesus Christ our Lord.

MISSIONARIES

COLLECT

Everlasting God,
whose servant *N* carried the good news of your Son
    to the people of . . .

grant that we who commemorate his/her service
may know the hope of the gospel in our hearts
and manifest its light in all our ways;
through Jesus Christ your Son our Lord,
who is alive and reigns with you
in the unity of the Holy Spirit,
one God, now and for ever.

POST-COMMUNION PRAYER

Holy Father, who gathered us here around the table of
    your Son
to share this meal with the whole household of God:
in that new world where you reveal
    the fullness of your peace,
gather people of every race and language
to share with N and all your saints
in the eternal banquet of Jesus Christ our Lord.

ANY SAINT

COLLECT

Almighty Father,
you have built up your Church
through the love and devotion of your saints:
inspire us to follow the example of N,
whom we commemorate today,
that we in our generation may rejoice with him/her
in the vision of your glory;
through Jesus Christ your Son our Lord,
who is alive and reigns with you
in the unity of the Holy Spirit,
one God, now and for ever.

or (for Christian rulers)

Sovereign God,
who called N to be a ruler among his/her people
and gave him/her grace to be their servant:
help us, following our Saviour Christ

in the path of humble service,
to see his kingdom set forward on earth
and to enjoy its fullness in heaven;
who is alive and reigns with you
in the unity of the Holy Spirit,
one God, now and for ever.

or (for those working for the poor and underprivileged)

Merciful God,
you have compassion on all that you have made
and your whole creation is enfolded in your love:
help us to stand firm for your truth,
to struggle against poverty
and to share your love with our neighbour,
that with your servant *N*
we may be instruments of your peace;
through Jesus Christ your Son our Lord,
who is alive and reigns with you
in the unity of the Holy Spirit,
one God, now and for ever.

or (for men and women of learning)

God our Father,
who gave wisdom and insight to your servant *N*
to fathom the depths of your love
and to understand your design for the world you have made:
grant us the help of your Holy Spirit
that we also may come to a full knowledge of your purposes
revealed in your Son Jesus Christ, our Wisdom and our Life;
who is alive and reigns with you
in the unity of the Holy Spirit,
one God, now and for ever.

*or (for those whose holiness was revealed in marriage and
family life)*

Eternal God,
whose love is revealed in the mystery of the Trinity:
help us, like your servant *N*,
to find in our human loving a mirror of your divine love
and to see in all your children our brothers and sisters
    in Christ,

who is alive and reigns with you
in the unity of the Holy Spirit,
one God, now and for ever.

POST-COMMUNION PRAYER

Faithful God,
who called *N* to serve you
and gave him/her joy in walking the path of holiness:
by this eucharist
in which you renew within us the vision of your glory,
strengthen us all to follow the way of perfection
until we come to see you face to face;
through Jesus Christ our Lord.

or

God our Redeemer,
who inspired *N* to witness to your love
and to work for the coming of your kingdom:
may we, who in this sacrament share the bread of heaven,
be fired by your Spirit to proclaim the gospel in our daily living
and never to rest content until your kingdom come,
on earth as in heaven;
through Jesus Christ our Lord.

or

Father,
from whom every family in heaven and on earth takes its name,
your servant *N* revealed your goodness
in a life of tranquillity and service:
grant that we who have gathered in faith around this table
may like him/her know the love of Christ
that surpasses knowledge
and be filled with all your fullness;
through Jesus Christ our Lord.

or

God, the source of all holiness
and giver of all good things:
may we who have shared at this table
as strangers and pilgrims here on earth
be welcomed with all your saints
to the heavenly feast on the day of your kingdom;
through Jesus Christ our Lord.

Special Occasions

_____ Special Occasions _____

MOTHERING SUNDAY

See page 181.

—

THE GUIDANCE OF THE HOLY SPIRIT

COLLECT

God, who from of old taught the hearts of your faithful people
by sending to them the light of your Holy Spirit:
grant us by the same Spirit
to have a right judgement in all things
and evermore to rejoice in his holy comfort;
through the merits of Christ Jesus our Saviour,
who is alive and reigns with you
in the unity of the Holy Spirit,
one God, now and for ever.

_or_

Almighty God,
you have given your Holy Spirit to the Church
to lead us into all truth:
bless with the Spirit's grace and presence
   the members of this . . . (_synod/PCC/etc._);
keep us/them steadfast in faith and united in love,
that we/they may manifest your glory
and prepare the way of your kingdom;

through Jesus Christ your Son our Lord,
who is alive and reigns with you
in the unity of the Holy Spirit,
one God, now and for ever.

POST-COMMUNION PRAYER

God of power,
whose Holy Spirit renews your people
in the bread and wine we bless and share:
may the boldness of the Spirit transform us,
the gentleness of the Spirit lead us,
and the gifts of the Spirit equip us
    to serve and worship you;
through Jesus Christ our Lord.

ROGATION DAYS

COLLECT

Almighty God,
whose will it is that the earth and the sea
    should bear fruit in due season:
bless the labours of those who work on land and sea,
grant us a good harvest
and the grace always to rejoice in your fatherly care;
through Jesus Christ your Son our Lord,
who is alive and reigns with you
in the unity of the Holy Spirit,
one God, now and for ever.

or

Almighty God and Father,
you have so ordered our life
   that we are dependent on one another:
prosper those engaged in commerce and industry
and direct their minds and hands
that they may rightly use your gifts in the service of others;
through Jesus Christ your Son our Lord,
who is alive and reigns with you
 in the unity of the Holy Spirit,
one God, now and for ever.

or

God our Father,
you never cease the work you have begun
and prosper with your blessing all human labour:
make us wise and faithful stewards of your gifts
that we may serve the common good,
maintain the fabric of our world
and seek that justice where all may share
   the good things you pour upon us;
through Jesus Christ your Son our Lord,
who is alive and reigns with you
in the unity of the Holy Spirit,
one God, now and for ever.

POST-COMMUNION PRAYER

God our creator,
you give seed for us to sow and bread for us to eat:
as you have blessed the fruit of our labour in this eucharist,
so we ask you to give all your children their daily bread,
that the world may praise you for your goodness;
through Jesus Christ our Lord.

HARVEST THANKSGIVING

COLLECT

Eternal God,
you crown the year with your goodness
and you give us the fruits of the earth in their season:
grant that we may use them to your glory,
for the relief of those in need and for our own well-being;
through Jesus Christ your Son our Lord,
who is alive and reigns with you
in the unity of the Holy Spirit,
one God, now and for ever.

POST-COMMUNION PRAYER

Lord of the harvest,
with joy we have offered thanksgiving
　　for your love in creation
and have shared in the bread and the wine of the kingdom:
by your grace plant within us a reverence
　　for all that you give us
and make us generous and wise stewards
of the good things we enjoy;
through Jesus Christ our Lord.

THE PEACE OF THE WORLD

COLLECT

Almighty God,
from whom all thoughts of truth and peace proceed:
kindle, we pray, in the hearts of all, the true love of peace
and guide with your pure and peaceable wisdom
those who take counsel for the nations of the earth
that in tranquillity your kingdom may go forward,
till the earth is filled with the knowledge of your love;

through Jesus Christ your Son our Lord,
who is alive and reigns with you
in the unity of the Holy Spirit,
one God, now and for ever.

POST-COMMUNION PRAYER

God our Father,
your Son is our peace
and his cross the sign of reconciliation:
help us, who share the broken bread,
to bring together what is scattered
and to bind up what is wounded,
that Christ may bring in the everlasting kingdom of his peace;
who is alive and reigns, now and for ever.

SOCIAL JUSTICE AND RESPONSIBILITY

COLLECT

Eternal God,
in whose perfect realm
no sword is drawn but the sword of righteousness,
and no strength known but the strength of love:
so guide and inspire the work of those who seek your kingdom
that all your people may find their security
in that love which casts out fear
and in the fellowship revealed to us
in Jesus Christ our Saviour,
who is alive and reigns with you
in the unity of the Holy Spirit,
one God, now and for ever.

or

Almighty and eternal God,
to whom we must all give account:
guide with your Spirit the . . . of this (*city/society/etc.*)
that we/they may be faithful to the mind of Christ
and seek in all our/their purposes to enrich our common life;

through Jesus Christ your Son our Lord,
who is alive and reigns with you
in the unity of the Holy Spirit,
one God, now and for ever.

POST-COMMUNION PRAYER

Blessed God,
help us, whom you have fed and satisfied in this eucharist,
to hunger and thirst for what is right;
help us, who here have rejoiced and been glad,
to stand with those who are persecuted and reviled;
help us, who here have glimpsed the life of heaven,
to strive for the cause of right
and for the coming of the kingdom of Jesus Christ,
who is alive and reigns, now and for ever.

THE UNITY OF THE CHURCH

COLLECT

Heavenly Father,
you have called us in the Body of your Son Jesus Christ
to continue his work of reconciliation
and reveal you to the world:
forgive us the sins which tear us apart;
give us the courage to overcome our fears
and to seek that unity which is your gift and your will;
through Jesus Christ your Son our Lord,
who is alive and reigns with you
in the unity of the Holy Spirit,
one God, now and for ever.

or

Lord Jesus Christ,
who said to your apostles,
'Peace I leave with you, my peace I give to you':
look not on our sins but on the faith of your Church
and grant it the peace and unity of your kingdom;
where you are alive and reign with the Father
in the unity of the Holy Spirit,
one God, now and for ever.

POST-COMMUNION PRAYER

Eternal God and Father,
whose Son at supper prayed that his disciples might be one,
as he is one with you:
draw us closer to him,
that in common love and obedience to you
we may be united to one another
in the fellowship of the one Spirit,
that the world may believe that he is Lord,
    to your eternal glory;
through Jesus Christ our Lord.

MISSION AND EVANGELISM

COLLECT

Almighty God,
who called your Church to witness
that you were in Christ reconciling the world to yourself:
help us so to proclaim the good news of your love,
that all who hear it may be drawn to you;
through him who was lifted up on the cross,
and reigns with you
in the unity of the Holy Spirit,
one God, now and for ever.

POST-COMMUNION PRAYER

Eternal God, giver of love and power,
your Son Jesus Christ has sent us into all the world
to preach the good news of his kingdom:
confirm us in this mission
and help us to live the good news we proclaim;
through Jesus Christ our Lord.

MINISTRY
including Ember Days

COLLECT

(for the ministry of all Christian people)

Almighty and everlasting God,
by whose Spirit the whole body of the Church
   is governed and sanctified:
hear our prayer which we offer for all your faithful people,
that in their vocation and ministry
they may serve you in holiness and truth
to the glory of your name;
through our Lord and Saviour Jesus Christ,
who is alive and reigns with you
in the unity of the Holy Spirit,
one God, now and for ever.

or (for those to be ordained)

Almighty God, the giver of all good gifts,
by your Holy Spirit you have appointed
   various orders of ministry in the Church:
look with mercy on your servants
   now called to be deacons and priests;
maintain them in truth and renew them in holiness,
that by word and good example they may faithfully serve you
to the glory of your name and the benefit of your Church;
through the merits of our Saviour Jesus Christ,
who is alive and reigns with you

in the unity of the Holy Spirit,
one God, now and for ever.

or (for vocations)

Almighty God,
you have entrusted to your Church
a share in the minsitry of your Son our great High Priest:
inspire by your Holy Spirit the hearts of many
to offer themselves for the ministry of your Church,
that strengthened by his power,
they may work for the increase of your kingdom
and set forward the eternal praise of your name;
through Jesus Christ your Son our Lord,
who is alive and reigns with you
in the unity of the Holy Spirit,
one God, now and for ever.

or (for the inauguration of a new ministry)

God our Father; Lord of all the world,
through your Son you have called us
    into the fellowship of your universal Church:
hear our prayer for your faithful people
that in their vocation and ministry
each may be an instrument of your love,
and give to your servant *N* now to be . . .
    (*installed, inducted etc.*)
the needful gifts of grace;
through our Lord and Saviour Jesus Christ,
who is alive and reigns with you
in the unity of the Holy Spirit,
one God, now and for ever.

POST-COMMUNION PRAYER

Heavenly Father,
whose ascended Son gave gifts of leadership and service
    to the Church:
strengthen us who have received this holy food
to be good stewards of your manifold grace,
through him who came not to be served but to serve,
and to give his life as a ransom for many,
Jesus Christ our Lord.

or

Lord of the harvest,
you have fed your people in this sacrament
with the fruits of creation made holy by your Spirit:
by your grace raise up among us faithful labourers
to sow your word and reap the harvest of souls;
through Jesus Christ our Lord.

IN TIME OF TROUBLE

COLLECT

Sovereign God,
the defence of those who trust in you
and the strength of those who suffer:
look with mercy on our affliction
and deliver us through our mighty Saviour Jesus Christ,
who is alive and reigns with you
in the unity of the Holy Spirit,
one God, now and for ever.

POST-COMMUNION PRAYER

Almighty God,
whose Son gave us in this meal a pledge of your saving love
and a foretaste of your kingdom of justice and peace:
strengthen your people in their faith
that they may endure the sufferings of this present time
in expectation of the glory to be revealed;
through Jesus Christ our Lord.

FOR THE SOVEREIGN

COLLECT

Almighty God, the fountain of all goodness,
bless our Sovereign Lady, Queen Elizabeth,
and all who are put in authority under her;
that they may order all things
    in wisdom and equity, righteousness and peace,
to the honour and glory of your name
and the good of your Church and people;
through Jesus Christ your Son our Lord,
who is alive and reigns with you
in the unity of the Holy Spirit,
one God, now and for ever.

POST-COMMUNION PRAYER

O God, the Father of our Lord Jesus Christ,
our only Saviour, the Prince of Peace:
give us grace seriously to lay to heart
the great dangers we are in by our unhappy divisions;
take away our hatred and prejudice
and whatever else may hinder us from godly union
    and concord,
that, as there is but one body, one Spirit
and one hope of our calling,
one Lord, one faith, one baptism,
one God and Father of us all,
so may we henceforth be all of one heart and of one soul,
united in one holy bond of truth and peace, of faith
    and charity,
and may with one mind and one mouth glorify you;
through Jesus Christ our Lord.

The Society for Promoting Christian Knowledge (SPCK) was founded in 1698. It has as its purpose three main tasks:

- **Communicating the Christian faith in its rich diversity**

- **Helping people to understand the Christian faith and to develop their personal faith**

- **Equipping Christians for mission and ministry**

SPCK Worldwide serves the Church through Christian literature and communication projects in over 100 countries. Special schemes also provide books for those training for ministry in many parts of the developing world. SPCK Worldwide's ministry involves Churches of many traditions. This worldwide service depends upon the generosity of others and all gifts are spent wholly on ministry programmes, without deductions.

SPCK Bookshops support the life of the Christian community by making available a full range of Christian literature and other resources, and by providing support to bookstalls and book agents throughout the UK. SPCK Bookshops' mail order department meets the needs of overseas customers and those unable to have access to local bookshops.

SPCK Publishing produces Christian books and resources, covering a wide range of inspirational, pastoral, practical and academic subjects. Authors are drawn from many different Christian traditions, and publications aim to meet the needs of a wide variety of readers in the UK and throughout the world.

The Society does not necessarily endorse the individual views contained in its publications, but hopes they stimulate readers to think about and further develop their Christian faith.

For further information about the Society, please write to:
SPCK, Holy Trinity Church, Marylebone Road,
London NW1 4DU, United Kingdom.
Telephone: 0171 387 5282